THE JOYS OF COLLECTING

General view of J. Paul Getty's home in Malibu, California, U.S.A.

THE JOYS OF COLLECTING

BY

J. PAUL GETTY

with additional text by
JEAN CHARBONNEAUX
Member of the Institut de France
and Keeper of Antiquities in the Louvre, Paris,
Translated from the French by Richard Miller

JULIUS S. HELD
Professor of Art History,
Barnard College, Columbia University,
New York City, and

PIERRE VERLET
Chief Keeper of the Department
of Furniture and Objets d'art,
Louvre, Paris
Translated from the French by Richard Miller

HAWTHORN BOOKS, INC. *Publishers,* New York

 Library of Congress Catalogue Card Number: 65-22891.

First Edition November, 1965

H–5295

This book was designed by
JEANNE LAMY
JEAN-DOMINIQUE REY
with the co-operation of the authors
and the assistance of William Voelkle
for the chapter on paintings.
The photograph of J. Paul Getty
reproduced on page 6 is by JEAN VINCENT,
Paris. All the other illustrations have been provided
by the J. Paul Getty Museum, Malibu, California.

⁂

NOTE

Some of the objects of art described and depicted in this book are still the personal property of Mr. J. Paul Getty. Others have been donated by him to the Los Angeles County Museum. Yet others have been donated to the J. Paul Getty Museum in Los Angeles, where they are on free display to the general public.

⁂

Printed in Germany by K.G. Lohse, Graphischer Großbetrieb, Frankfurt am Main

Contents

Sutton Place, Surrey, England, where J. Paul Getty has installed a port of his collection.

A WORD OF INTRODUCTION

It has long been my belief that some important generalizations may safely be made about art collectors and collecting.

First, I firmly believe that almost anyone can become a collector, and that he or she can start collecting at almost any period of life. One need not be an expert or have large amounts of time or money to start an art collection.

Second, I hold that few human activities provide an individual with a greater sense of personal gratification than the assembling of a collection of art objects that appeal to him and that he feels have true and lasting beauty.

Third, I maintain that the true worth of a collection cannot — and should not — be measured solely in terms of its monetary value. Artistic merit does not necessarily follow the values set in the market. Although price tags can be — and are — attached to works of art, the beauty an individual sees in an object and the pleasure and satisfaction he derives from possessing it cannot be accurately or even properly gauged exclusively in terms of dollars and cents.

Last, I am convinced that the true collector does not acquire objects of art for himself alone. His is no selfish drive or desire to have and hold a painting, a sculpture, or a fine example of antique furniture so that only he may see and enjoy it. Appreciating the beauty of the object, he is willing and even eager to have others share his pleasure. It is, of course, for this reason that so many collectors loan their finest pieces to museums or establish museums of their own where the items they have painstakingly collected may be viewed by the general public.

These generalizations go far toward explaining why I have approved the publication of this book, and written the text which immediately follows. At my request the world-famous art authorities. Jean Charbonneaux, Julius S. Held and Pierre Verlet have added their notes and comments to the contents of the volume.

My aim in writing *The Joys of Collecting* is an ambitious one. It is my desire to convey to the reader the romance and zest—the excitement, suspense, thrills and triumphs—that make art collecting one of the most exhilarating and satisfying of all human endeavors.

In my opinion, an individual without any love of the arts cannot be considered completely civilized. At the same time, it is extremely difficult, and sometimes impossible, to interest people in works of art unless they can see them and know something about them. It was for this reason that I established the J. Paul Getty Museum in Los Angeles a decade or so ago. A separate wing was built onto my home there to serve as a museum for the public. I am gradually giving my works of art to this museum.

In a manner of speaking, this book is an extension of the museum. It will enable many people who might never visit Southern California and the museum to see the beauty of the art objects it has been my good fortune to acquire, to know something about them and to understand the great joys I have experienced as a collector.

To those, collectors or not, who live in or near—or who may visit—Southern California, I extend a warm and sincere invitation to see the treasures I collected through the years and which are now displayed at the J. Paul Getty Museum. It is located on the Pacific Coast Highway in Malibu. The museum is open to the public, and admission is free.

I would also like here to express my deep gratitude to those who during my collecting days so kindly helped me with their connoisseurship and learning, particularly to Colin Agnew, Bernard Berenson, John Brealey, Gerald Brockhurst, Jean Charbonneaux, Ludwig Curtius, Edward Fowles, Cecil Gould, Julius Held, Sir Philip Hendy, Leon Lacroix, Philip Pouncey, Stephen Rees Jones, Mitchell Samuels, Alfred Scharf, W. Valentiner, Pierre Verlet, Francis Watson, Paul Wescher and Federico Zeri. I was their earnest and grateful student whenever I was fortunate enough to be with them, and this has added greatly to my appreciation of art and my joys of collecting.

I particularly want to thank Jean Charbonneaux, Julius S. Held and Pierre Verlet for having added their invaluable and authoritative comments.

It is my earnest hope that this book will bring pleasure and be of interest and some assistance to those who are interested in the categories of art with which it is concerned.

I also hope that the account of my experiences as a collector will prove of some help and, perhaps, encouragement to other collectors, and especially those who would like to collect but, for whatever reasons, hesitate to do so.

I think that much of the hesitancy of the would-be collector will vanish if he simply bears in mind that every collector was once a beginner.

To the art lovers who have taken—or who will take—the first step, I extend my heartiest congratulations, for they will greatly enrich their lives.

I.

On July 20, 1938, I was in London attending an auction at Sotheby's. At that time, Europe was already moving steadily closer to the brink of World War II. Civil war was raging in Spain. Italy had withdrawn from the League of Nations. Adolf Hitler had repudiated the Treaty of Versailles, annexed Austria and was making demands for the cession of Czechoslovakian territory to Nazi Germany.

Most Londoners felt there was little question that a general conflict was near and that, although the holocaust might perhaps be temporarily postponed, it could not be indefinitely averted.

I could sense the tension and gloom, the fear of impending disaster, wherever I went in the British capital.

Hence, it was hardly surprising that, while the sale at Sotheby's was fairly well attended, it had an almost desultory air about it. There was little of the customary subdued, but nonetheless electric, excitement to the bidding. Many of those attending seemed deeply preoccupied, lost in the contemplation of decisions being made and events taking place far away and beyond their control.

As an American — remember this was in mid-1938, more than three years before Pearl Harbor — I could sympathize with, but not quite share the feelings of the people who sat around me. Like the vast majority of my countrymen at that time, I was not fully alert to the dangers threatening the world. My attention was thus not distracted from less important and more immediate matters. I was at Sotheby's because I wanted to bid on several items that were listed in the sale catalog, which, incidentally, bore a cover announcement that would make any serious collector's mouth water:

> Sotheby's Sale of Celebrated Paintings comprising the Collections of The Royal House of France removed from Schloss Frohsdorf, Lower Austria and now sold by order of H. R. H. Princess Beatrix de Bourbon-Massimo.

The paintings being offered were from the collection of the late Jaime III of Bourbon. Many of them had originally been in the Tuileries, but were removed to the Castle Frohsdorf, which became the home of the Bourbons after their exile following the Revolution of 1830. The auction had been ordered by Princess Beatrix, the niece and heiress of Jaime III.

The day before the sale, I examined the paintings that were to be offered, and I became interested in four that were to be sold in three lots. Lot No. 30 consisted of two flower pieces attributed to Van Huysum.

The other two Lots — 49 and 136 — were of particular interest to me. The former was one of three "after-Raphael" paintings listed. These were Lot No. 48: The *Madonna del Passegio;* No. 49: The *Madonna of Loreto;* and No. 50: *The Holy Family (La Perla).* Lot No. 136 was a large, 144- by 64-inch Rigaud portrait of Louis XIV.

I decided I needed some expert advice before bidding on the *Madonna of Loreto* and the Louis XIV portrait. Gerald Brockhurst, the well-known English portraitist — who, I might add, painted my own portrait that same year — acted as my adviser in regard to the *Madonna.* He recommended that I purchase the panel, for he strongly suspected that it was not simply an "after-Raphael" painting; he believed the foreshortening of the Virgin's right arm betrayed the master's own touch.

Leon Lacroix, an expert on French eighteenth century art, gave me his opinion on Lot No. 136, the Louis XIV portrait. He thought it a good example of Rigaud's work.

And so I decided to buy, if I could, both these paintings. I really didn't have any set price limit in mind. I think that nearly all the art dealers of London and Paris, as well as numerous museum experts and private collectors, were present at the sale, and I expected stiff competition in the bidding.

As the sale progressed, it became apparent that those present were not inclined to pay high prices. When Lot No. 30—the flower pieces attributed to Van Huysum—was auctioned I bought it with a top bid of 55 pounds, in those days approximately $275.

A few minutes later, Lot No. 49 came up for sale. It was a panel that seemed unprepossessing at first glance. In fact, it was in a somewhat poor condition. It dealt with a classic subject, a portrait of the Holy Family. No special claims were made for it. The painting, it seemed, was a copy of Raphael's famed, long-lost *Madonna of Loreto.* It might have been executed by one of Raphael's students or contemporaries. Apparently no one else attending the sale had anything approaching my interest in the panel, and evidently none had seen what Gerald Brockhurst had noticed in the painting.

I waited for the opening bid, which proved to be 10 pounds, or about $50. By then an experienced and cautious auction buyer, I increased the bid only slightly, which someone promptly topped by another few pounds. And so it went, back and forth, until I bid 40 pounds—roughly $200—and there was no further competition. Lot No. 49 was mine. My 40-pound bid was more than anyone else was willing to pay.

My luck held when Lot No. 136 was offered. I purchased Rigaud's portrait of Louis XIV with a winning bid of 145 pounds (about $725). Soon afterward, I had the items I had purchased at various auctions shipped to New York.

My liking for the "after-Raphael" panel continued to grow after it was in my possession. I was constantly drawn to it, intrigued by it. And, I had confidence in it. To employ a colloquialism, the painting "had something"—something which set it apart, a quality which exerted an ever increasing attraction and fascination.

Years — twenty-five to be exact — passed. Although my collection expanded greatly and I had been lucky enough to acquire several very important additions to it in the interim, the $200 *Madonna* remained one of my favorites. In 1963, I had the painting shipped to Sutton Place in England.

There were some abrasions of the original paint and there seemed to be thick daubs of repaint and discolored varnish covering the panel. A few days after the painting arrived at Sutton Place, Colin Agnew, the prominent London art dealer and expert in Italian Renaissance paintings, visited Sutton Place and I asked him to look at the *Madonna.*

He was not impressed by the work. Quite to the contrary. He asked a friend of mine why I had purchased it. When told that I thought it was a Raphael, Colin blinked.

"Who in the world ever sold *that* thing to Paul as a Raphael!" he exclaimed.

Colin did, however, suggest that the painting badly needed cleaning. I followed his advice and sent the panel to him to be cleaned, and when the work was finished the quality of the picture became more evident. At this point, Colin became convinced that the *Madonna of Loreto* was by the master's own hand.

Subsequently, on the advice of a leading art historian, I had the picture given a thorough "stripping." This involved removal of all or almost all of the repaint to reveal the original work. As a result, the great quality of the painting became evident. One could now definitely see the early sixteenth century work of the master, Raphael, free of the disfiguring repaint of later generations.

Colin Agnew consulted with Dr. Alfred Scharf, an authority on fifteenth and sixteent century Italian paintings. After meticulous study of the panel, Dr. Scharf accepted it as an autograph work of Raphael.

The discovery caused a very considerable stir throughout the art world. Other experts who have since examined the panel and the infra-red photographs and X-rays that were taken of it concurred with Dr. Scharf's verdict.

As these words are being written, the *Madonna of Loreto* is on display in the Raphael Room of the National Gallery in London, to which great museum I loaned the painting in February 1965. It hangs next to another masterpiece of the immortal Raphael — his *Aldobrandini Madonna.*

Insofar as the monetary value of the *Madonna of Loreto* is concerned, authenticated as a genuine Raphael, it is virtually priceless. It is insured today for 10,000 times the price I originally paid for it!

I cite this for the same reason that I began my narrative with the story of this painting — to highlight the excitement and drama inherent in collecting and to demonstrate as forcibly as possible that there is often high adventure in collecting art. No matter how modestly he begins, there are no fixed limits or ceilings to halt or hinder the collector.

My own career as an art collector is, in many ways, a fairly illustrative case.

My interest in fine art was slow in awakening; my interest in actually collecting art was even slower.

I made my first visit to Europe with my mother and father in 1909. As part of our tour, we visited the Louvre in Paris and the National Gallery in London. Neither of these fabulous museums made much of an impression on me; perhaps I was still too young to appreciate what I saw.

Three years later, I returned to Europe — or, rather, to England, where I enrolled as a student at Oxford University. University regulations required me to be in residence for three six-week terms during the year. The remainder of the time, I was free to do very much as I pleased. I chose to travel.

I was a good, almost a model Cook's tourist. I faithfully made the rounds of the museums and galleries. Even so, my love of fine art still seemed to be dormant. I can recall being impressed by only one painting, that of *Venus* by Titian in the Uffizi in Florence.

Incidentally, in May and June of 1912, I had made a trip to China and Japan. I suppose that if one stretched the point almost to breaking, it could be said I started my collection during this visit to the Orient. I purchased my first art objects, two Chinese bronzes and some pieces of carved ivory. I seriously doubt that I paid much more than the equivalent of fifty dollars for the entire lot.

It was a timid and faltering start. The seeds of the urge to collect took an unseemly long time to sprout. Eighteen years were to pass before I resumed collecting again.

True, there were many totally unrelated forces and factors that served to inhibit my activities in these directions. Returning to the United States after obtaining a diploma in economics and political science at Oxford, I began wildcatting for oil in Oklahoma. Not until early 1916 did I bring in my first producing oil well, and from then on, except for a lull of less than a year, I devoted my time and energies to building and expanding my business enterprises.

Nevertheless, I found my interest in art growing and developing. I read voraciously on the subject and visited museums and galleries during my infrequent periods of leisure or holiday, not because these were the "things to do," but because I truly enjoyed doing them. Paradoxically, the more I learned, the more my knowledge served to dampen any inclination I may have had for collecting.

In the mid and late 1920s, very few works of art of good quality were to be found on the market. The best examples of almost all forms of fine art were in museums, huge private collections, or held by very strong hands.

The United States was enjoying a period of tremendous prosperity, and there were great numbers of extremely wealthy men in Britain and Europe. They bid against each other for whatever came on the market. Prices on those items that were available spiraled completely out of proportion to any reasonable scale of values.

Although I had achieved a degree of business success, I was certainly in no position to compete with collectors of the caliber of the Hearsts, Mellons or Rothschilds. Besides, since my business enterprises were still expanding, I reinvested most of my profits in them. I had only relatively small sums of ready cash at my disposal.

Withal, in the late 1920s, it appeared to me that the days of collecting were just about over. The men who had made their millions and tens of millions before I'd started in business—or even before I was born—swept up just about everything worthwhile that had found its way to the market over the past few decades. The old aristocratic British and European families who still possessed treasure troves of fine art were, for the most part, very well situated financially in those days. And, even if they were not and decided to sell an item or two, they had been conditioned to the idea of entertaining only the most staggering offers for their possessions.

The entire situation changed with awful suddenness. The great panic—the "Crash" —of 1929 shook the art world no less than it did the financial world. The 1930s brought no convincing recovery.

The Depression settled over the United States and spread to Britain and Europe. Now, many of the strong hands that formerly held some of the finest examples of art on the face of the earth were forced to relax their grip. Many choice items became available for purchase, and art prices, like all other prices of the time, dropped to levels which would have been inconceivable a few years or even months earlier.

Here was an opportunity for the would-be collector with comparatively limited means, which could not possibly have been foreseen before 1929. As I became aware of this, my long-dormant urge to collect things of beauty and examples of fine art finally awoke.

In 1930 I bought a painting by Van Goyen for about $1,100. By 1932 I was actively acquiring paintings, sculptures and other works of art of museum quality.

I continued collecting until 1964, when I more or less stopped. I felt that I had acquired enough, that I had assembled a collection of which I could be proud—and that I should leave the field to others.

My collecting over the years has been a labor of love and, I believe, it might make a story worth telling.

II.

At some point or another, preferably as early as possible, the collector must make up his mind what it is precisely he wishes to collect. The decision can lie anywhere between two widely separated extremes.

He may, for example, limit his collection solely to bronzes of a certain period or even of a specific century and national origin. At the other extreme, he may conceivably emulate the late William Randolph Hearst who literally collected everything from prehistoric figurines and old masters to castles and their entire contents.

The choice a collector makes is necessarily guided and governed by many and various factors and influences. The most important consideration is, of course, the simplest one of all: in what direction or directions do his interests in and liking for fine art lie?

What is the ultimate in artistic beauty to one person, may well be a bore or an abomination to another. This should be obvious to anyone who has ever watched any sizeable group of people making its way through a large museum.

There are those in the group who will glance at a Goya and give a disinterested yawn, but who will stand transfixed, gazing with awe at a Gauguin. To some, Bernini is an anathema, while Rodin is sublime. There are individuals who respond enthusiastically to Venetian Settecento furniture but remain completely unmoved by the finest examples of the eighteenth-century French cabinetmakers' art.

And so it goes.

The variations and differences between individual tastes, likes and dislikes are infinite in regard to almost everything in life. When it comes to fine art, individual tastes and preferences become even more pronounced—this is especially so with collectors.

Possibly, it is as Aline B. Saarinen has said, that for the true collector, "the collecting of art [is] a primary means of expression." Without doubt, the collector reflects much of his innermost self, his convictions, attitudes and outlooks in what he collects.

My own philosophy regarding my collection can be summed up by a paragraph Ethel Le Vane wrote in the book, *Collector's Choice,* a decade ago:

> To me, my works of art are all vividly alive. They are the embodiment of whoever created them—a mirror of their creator's hopes, dreams and frustrations. They have led eventful lives—pampered by the aristocracy and pillaged by revolution, courted with ardor and cold-bloodedly abandoned. They have been honored by drawing rooms and humbled by attics. So many worlds in their life-span, yet all were transitory. Their worlds have long since disintegrated, yet they live on—and, for the most part, they are as beautiful as ever.

Banal as it may sound in this glib and brittle age, the beauty that one finds in fine art is one of the pitifully few real and lasting products of all human endeavor. That beauty endures even though nations and civilizations crumble; the work of art can be passed on from generation to generation and century to century, providing a historical continuity of true value.

When I began to collect actively, I determined to keep my collection comparatively small and to purchase only items of the highest artistic quality and merit. I felt that I would much rather own a few choice pieces than to amass an agglomeration of second-rate items. I also resolved to concentrate on certain schools, largely limiting myself to those that I liked best and interested me most. Therefore, the majority of my collection consists of the following categories:

> Greek and Roman marbles and bronzes; Renaissance paintings; sixteenth-century Persian carpets; Savonnerie carpets and eighteenth-century French furniture and tapestries.

I have, of course, made several exceptions and digressions. It might, I think, be interesting to the reader, and amusing in at least one instance if I touched upon the circumstances surrounding some of these digressions before continuing with the story of my collection proper.

As an example, I recall one purely accidental and unintentional purchase I made at Christie's a few years ago. The day was warm and the auction rooms were terribly crowded. For some unknown reason, no one had thought to open any windows. The atmosphere inside gradually became hotter and stickier, eventually to such a degree that I was completely distracted from the sale then in progress. A friend sat next to me and also suffered from the heat and lack of fresh air.

"You'd think the staff would do something about the ventilation in here," he commented to me *sotto voce.*

I nodded agreement and unconsciously reached up to loosen my shirt-collar. A moment later, I noticed the auctioneer pointing directly at me.

"Yours, sir — for one hundred guineas!" he announced loudly.

I blinked at him in astonishment. For several seconds I was completely baffled and then I realized what had happened. While I had been fretting about the ventilation and paying no attention to the sale, a painting was being auctioned. The bidding had reached the point at which the auctioneer was asking, "Will anyone offer a hundred guineas?"

Now, art auctions have their etiquette. Buyers seldom call out their bids. They "telegraph" them through surreptitious movements of their hands or heads, by a flick of the catalog they hold or some other, similar means. Veteran auctioneers are constantly alert for such signals.

Thus, when for the third time, Christie's auctioneer had asked if anyone would offer one hundred guineas for the item then being offered and I made as if to loosen the collar of my shirt, he took it as a signal that I was willing to pay the price.

My consternation quickly became apparent to all those seated near me and occasioned much sympathetic laughter. I laughed, too. There was nothing to do but accept the situation with good grace, and I consequently became the owner of what was listed in the sale catalog as "No. 18-A: A watercolor of old London about 1845."

The circumstances surrounding another of my digressions as a collector were far different. In November 1933 I attended the Thomas Fortune Ryan sale at the Anderson Galleries in New York City. There I purchased a total of twelve pieces. Ten were paintings by the Spanish Impressionist Joaquin Sorolla y Bastida, who died in 1923. Obviously, his work did not fit any of the five major categories into which I intended to channel my collecting efforts.

However, I was struck by the remarkable quality of Sorolla's paintings, being especially fascinated by his unique treatment of sunlight. I bid in the ten canvasses and the two other items I bought during the sale for an overall price of considerably less than $10,000. I have never had any cause to regret my decision.

Looking at the acquisition from an investment standpoint, it was a highly fortuitous one. By 1938 the monetary value of the ten Sorollas had risen to $ 40,000.

Although the purchase of these Impressionist works was a major digression from my usual fivefold collecting path, my opinion regarding their beauty, appeal and artistic merit remains the same as it was when I first saw the canvasses.

I have made other exceptions to my general five-category rule. Among them are some excellent English portraits by Gainsborough and Romney. One Gainsborough has been described as "one of the really great English portraits" by no less an authority than Dr. Julius S. Held, professor of art history at Barnard College, Columbia University. There is, I might add, a tinge of irony in the fact that I own it. The portrait is of James A. Christie, founder of Christie, Manson and Woods, the world-famous London auction-gallery generally known as Christie's.

The portrait was painted in 1778, when James A. Christie was 48. It was immediately recognized as one of Gainsborough's finer works and was exhibited at the Royal Academy in London in 1778, 1817 and 1859, and subsequently at several other major exhibitions.

How and why the Christie family, steeped for generations in knowledge and appreciation of fine art, permitted this exceptional work and priceless heirloom to slip out of its hands is an unfathomable mystery. However, in 1927 it was sold—at Christie's—for 7,560 pounds sterling. The purchaser was Thomas Agnew & Sons, another art dealer. In 1938, I bought it from Colnaghi's Gallery for 7,500 pounds. It was, incidentally, one of a group of paintings that I loaned to the New York World's Fair for exhibition in 1939. Another was Rembrandt's *Portrait of Marten Looten,* which has a fascinating history about which I shall have more to say later.

In recent years, I have, on occasion, wandered even farther afield in my collecting. Among my acquisitions have been two fine works by Edgar Degas, each of which brilliantly demonstrates an entirely different facet of his genius. The first is *Sea-Side Landscape*—indeed a rarity, for Degas devoted the majority of his work to scenes from the theater and ballet. It was only during a comparatively brief period of his long career that he produced a handful of canvasses and pastels inspired by the sea. My other Degas, *Three Dancers in Pink,* is an excellent representative example of his traditional work. As the title implies, it depicts a trio of female dancers, and the composition, color and treatment give the canvas a throbbing, vital quality.

Another purchase was a painting by Claude Monet, *The Cliffs of Pourville in the Morning.* Painted near Dieppe in 1897, this is a work to which Monet imparted a deeply moving lyrical quality by bathing the scene in a tremulous blue light.

Landscape Near Rouen by Paul Gauguin is also a comparatively recent "offbeat" addition to my collection. It is a lovely work and unusual for at least two reasons: As an early Gauguin—it was painted in 1884, six years before he set up his studio in Tahiti—it has a very pronounced Impressionistic quality. Second, there are very few Gauguin landscapes extant that do not date from his Brittany period or from the time he stayed in Provence. An added feature of interest is the inscription that appears on the painting: "*A mon ami* William Lund."

In 1956 I purchased Auguste Renoir's jewel-like *The Village of Essoyes.* This is a small canvas, scarcely 10 by 12 inches in size, but it is an exquisite painting of the village in the Aube for which the artist bore such great love and to which he had such a strong attachment. It was the birthplace of his wife and his famed model Gabrielle. Renoir bought a house there and spent many of his summers in it. It was in Essoyes during the summer months that he received an endless flow of visitors, among them a great many of the younger painters of the period who where influenced by him and later made their own reputations in the world of art.

Finally, I would like to mention just one more of my latter-day digressions, Pierre Bonnard's *Woman in the Nude*. "Strikingly composed," is Dr. Julius Held's comment on this large (approximately 54 by 31 inches) painting by Bonnard who, with Edouard Vuillard, had such a profound influence on the direction painting took in the post-Impressionist period.

Obviously, I have deviated far from my main theme — the body of my collection — even before making a proper beginning. But first, I chose to dispose of the exceptions to my self-imposed rules governing the categories of art I had decided to collect, for a reason. The few representative digressions I have described serve to illustrate that even the collector who is grimly determined to specialize or limit himself is highly likely to be led, or to lead himself, down many detours and byways.

Although he may prefer one or a few types or schools of art to all others, his acquaintance with and understanding of one or certain specific forms of beauty cannot help but extend and expand his aesthetic horizons. He cannot avoid, sooner or later, recognizing and appreciating other forms, other schools, other categories of fine art. As his specialized collection grows, so his tolerance, his understanding and appreciation will grow. And so will his depth and dimension as a perceptive, sensitive and well-rounded individual.

As may be seen from the Table of Contents, the plates and the accompanying discussions by Messsrs. Charbonneaux, Held and Verlet fall into three sections:

1. Greek and Roman antiquities.
2. Paintings.
3. Furniture and objets d'art.

I shall tell the story of my collection — and my collecting — in the same order.

III.

I have said that the collector frequently experiences thrills and sometimes savors triumphs. My "find" of Raphael's *Madonna of Loreto,* already mentioned — is an exemplary illustration of this. Equally great is the sense of triumph a collector experiences when he succeeds in acquiring a unique work of exceptional artistic and historical value that he and the entire art world have long believed to be absolutely unobtainable at any price.

It has been my immense good fortune to have had such experiences on several occasions during my career as a collector. Some of the more outstanding of these have occured in my collecting of Greek and Roman antiquities.

One of these exceptional triumphs was my totally unexpected — and theretofore completely undreamed of — success in obtaining the celebrated Lansdowne *Hercules* (or *Herakles*) for my collection.

There is evidence to suggest that this large (76¼ inches high) Pentelic marble statue was a great favorite of the Roman Emperor Hadrian, who was the most sophisticated of all ancient Roman emperors. It is a first-century B.C. — first-century A.D. Roman replica of a work by Scopas.

The statue was found in 1790 in the ruins of Hadrian's villa outside Rome. For a brief time, it was the property of an aristocratic Roman family, but in 1792 it was purchased by an English nobleman, the Marquis of Lansdowne, who paid 600 pounds sterling for it. He took the statue to England, where he was assembling a truly important collection of statuary in his luxurious Berkeley Square house.

The fame of the Lansdowne *Hercules* grew through the decades. It was generally conceded to be the finest piece in the entire Lansdowne collection and, in fact, one of the finest examples of classical statuary anywhere outside Greece or Italy.

Adolf Michaelis, the German-born archaeologist and leading authority on ancient marbles in Great Britain, pronounced the Lansdowne *Hercules* to be "perhaps the most important classical statue in English collections."

The *Hercules* has figured prominently and received the highest praise in the works of other leading experts, including Gisela Richter and Adolf Furtwängler.

The statue remained in possession of the Marquis of Lansdowne's descendants. Dealers and collectors alike assumed that is was untouchable, that the family could never be induced to part with it — or, at the very least, only at an astronomical price. They knew the Lansdowne family had sold another piece in the collection, *Wounded Amazon,* in 1930 when art prices were already depressed. This statue was considered inferior to the *Hercules,* but nonetheless, it was purchased for a staggering 28,000 pounds sterling (then nearly $140,000) by John D. Rockefeller, Jr. With such a precedent established, what offer, if any, would the Lansdowne family entertain for the fabulous *Hercules?* One dared not even think.

Then, one afternoon, I was browsing in Christie's. I chatted with the manager and invited him to have lunch with me the following day at the Ritz Hotel, where I was staying. During the course of the luncheon, I mentioned that I was in the market for ancient marbles. My companion's next remark practically stunned me.

"I would prefer not to be quoted," he said, "but I've heard rumors there might be a possibility of something being available from the Lansdowne Collection. As you doubtless know, the family deals mainly through Spink & Son."

My collector's instincts snapped to attention, and a sudden though only very faint hope arose. Could there possibly be a chance of obtaining the Lansdowne *Hercules*? I braced myself psychologically for what I was certain would be an eventual refusal and soon began the necessary diplomatic overtures to the Lansdowne family through Spink's. The negotiations were protracted, and there were several disheartening days when I was sure that I had failed.

At last, to my incredulous joy, the family made its decision—one, which for me, was fantastically favorable. Yes, I could have the Lansdowne *Hercules*, for the astounding price of 6,000 pounds, plus a 10 percent commission to Spink's. What was more, the family was willing to part with another piece, a Pentelic marble group of *Leda and the Swan* for only 500 pounds, plus Spink's commission.

Thus, the Lansdowne *Hercules* soon began its journey westward, to the United States. How Michaelis would rank the *Hercules* among the collections of classical statuary in the United States is something I do not know. It is enough for me to know that this magnificent marble sculpture, which once delighted the Emperor Hadrian and for a century and a half was a pride of Britain, is now completely "Americanized"—on view for all to see at the Getty Museum.

Another unforgettable triumph of my collecting career was my luck in obtaining three other "impossible" pieces, three of the world-famous Greek "Elgin Marbles" for my collection.

The "Elgin Marbles" as such have a fascinating history. It begins with Lord Thomas Bruce, 7th Earl of Elgin and 11th Earl of Kincardine, who during his lifetime (1766—1841) earned great distinction as a British diplomat and as an archaeologist. While serving as British Ambassador to the *Porte* (Greece was then part of the Ottoman Empire) Lord Elgin assembled a fabulous collection of pre-Christian Greek marbles, including the famed and breathtaking Parthenon frieze, and arranged for shipment of the collection to England.

The bulk of this collection, by far the finest of its kind anywhere in the world outside Greece, went into the British Museum, where it has since been viewed and marveled at by millions of people. Lord Duveen, the renowned art connoisseur and dealer, saw the collection many decades after Lord Elgin's death. He was so impressed that he donated a gallery to the British Museum—now known as "The Elgin Marbles Room" — so that the treasures could be displayed to best advantage.

Although the major portion of the marbles that Lord Elgin transported to England from Greece went to the British Museum, he retained a few pieces for his own private collection. For generations, they remained the property of his descendants, and it was virtually an article of faith among dealers and collectors that they would never, under any circumstances, become available.

Then one day while on a trip to Italy, I received a letter from Mrs. Ethel Le Vane. I read it and could scarcely believe what I read. The letter informed me in the strictest confidence that the 10th Earl of Elgin might — just *might* — be willing to sell three of the Elgin Marbles that remained in the family's possession. Would I be interested?

Would I! I wasted no time, but dispatched an affirmatory cable immediately. The three pieces in question were at Lord Elgin's ancestral mansion, Broom Hall, in Scotland. They consisted of the following:

1. *Myttion*, a fourth-century B.C. sepulchral stele representing the figure of a young girl with short, curly hair.

2. An Archaic *Kore*, or female figure, 28 inches high, made of Parian marble, of Attic origin and dating from the early fifth century B.C.

3. A sepulchral stele of Theogenis, Nikodemos and Nikomache dating from the early part of the fourth century B.C.

Needless to say, lengthy and delicate negotiations had to be made, export permits obtained and many other details attended to before the three precious pieces were mine. Withal, I was successful—and, as a collector, it was one of my great triumphs.

I derive much pride and satisfaction from my success in obtaining these three examples of the fabled Elgin Marbles and thus making it possible for my own countrymen to see and admire them in the J. Paul Getty Museum in Los Angeles.

In 1953 I paid a visit to that all-but-legendary figure of the art world, the late Bernard Berenson, at his villa I Tatti in Settignano, not far from Florence. Although I was aware that "B. B." did not particularly relish looking at photographs of works of art—a perfectionist, he wanted to see the actual object—I had brought along some photos of my Elgin Marbles and showed them to him. I was hardly prepared for his reaction when he saw the photograph of *Myttion.*

"Come over here and see something really great!" he exclaimed delightedly to one of his associates. "Now *this* is a piece I would love to have!"

For any collector, Bernard Berenson's enthusiastic response would have been a rare and special bounty and I was no exception.

Jean Charbonneaux, member of the Institute of France and Keeper of Antiquities at the Louvre, states that the Elgin *Kore* is one of the three rarest pieces in my collection of Greek and Roman antiquities. Another, he feels, is the Thasian bas-relief dating from the early fifth century B.C. that was found on Thasos in 1913 and which I obtained from the Wix de Szolnay collection. The third is the celebrated *Cottenham Relief,* which has a strange story of its own.

This Pentelic marble bas-relief—actually only an 11- by 12-inch top left-hand fragment of the original—dates from *circa* 500 B.C. It depicts a young man leading a horse by its bridle. The workmanship is exquisite.

"In this handsome fragment, all the grace of archaic Greek art is to be seen," says Charbonneaux.

The *Cottenham Relief* came to light in our present century, in 1911 to be exact, but it was not found in Greece. Paradoxically, it was discovered 18 inches beneath the surface of the ground, turned up by a laborer's pick, in England! The fragment was found in Cottenham, near Cambridge.

How did this sublime example of archaic Greek art reach England and become "lost" and "found" there? The precise details will never be known, but an entirely satisfactory skeleton of the explanation can be readily reconstructed.

Roger Gale (1672—1744), a noted antiquarian of his time, lived in the manor house at Cottenham in 1728. The fragment, or perhaps the entire original, almost certainly belonged to him. Somehow, possibly during the moving of his effects into or out of the house, the fragment was dropped on the ground or broke off the original. It is even within the realm of possibility that the fragment was left behind and thrown away by the subsequent occupants. In any event, it was trodden into the earth, where it remained until a laborer accidentally uncovered it nearly 200 years later.

It should hardly be necessary to say that by no means was every addition to my collection of Greek and Roman antiquities a triumph, and that by no means does every piece have such an odd recent history as the *Cottenham Relief.* Many of the items in the collection were acquired in the most prosaic way.

For example, my *Torso of Venus*—an almost life-size torso reputed to have been found in the sea at Anzio, not far from Nero's villa — was simply purchased from the Barsanti Galleries in Rome in 1939.

The Legend of Orpheus, a Gallo-Roman mosaic dating from the second or third century A.D., came into my possession via the William Randolph Hearst auction held at the Hammer Gallery in New York in 1941. This large mosaic (it measures 191$^{3}/_{4}$ inches by 139 inches) is intriguing for its intricate motifs and geometric designs. It was found in France, but is of Roman workmanship.

The fashion of constructing mosaic floors consisting of tiny colored stones and occasionally pieces of glass originated in the Orient. In Hellenistic times, it was particularly popular in Alexandria. Mosaic floors were introduced in Rome, other parts of Italy and in the Roman provinces during the Republican and later periods. High-ranking administrators and officials posted to the provinces frequently brought skilled artisans from Rome to construct mosaic floors for their villas.

When I purchased the mosaic at the Hearst sale, it had been cut into many sections and packed in crates. I decided to have it installed on top of the existing floor in what is now known as the "Roman Room" of the J. Paul Getty Museum.

I sought the advice of a firm that specialized in antique marbles. I was told that relaying an ancient mosaic floor was an intricate task of monumental proportions and that there were only a handful of skilled artisans in the United States capable of handling the task. The firm itself knew of only two such men — and several weeks were needed before one of them could be contacted. I had to bring him to Malibu from the East Coast, naturally paying all his traveling expenses.

The man's basic wage was five dollars an hour — and this was quite a number of years ago. He needed two months of painstaking labor, working eight hours a day, five days a week, to lay the mosaic floor. But it was well worth the cost, for he did a magnificent job. The mosaic floor depicting the *Legend of Orpheus,* which once graced some powerful Roman official's villa in Gaul, now provides a perfect decorative touch to the museum's Roman Room in which are displayed numerous Roman and some Hellenic antiquities I have collected.

So far, I have mentioned only some examples of marbles and, of course, the mosaic that are part of my Greek and Roman antiquities collection. I have also been fortunate to acquire some fine ancient bronzes. Among them is the statuette, *Phrixos,* a masterpiece of Polycletian style. It was originally in the Julius Böhler collection in Munich. Such is the rare quality of this bronze, that I gladly loaned it for exhibition to the Louvre for a few years.

M. Charbonneaux inclines to the belief that this *Phrixos* is a Greek original dating from the early fourth century B.C. He describes it as "very beautiful" and says "the statuette occupies an essential place in the history of this important period (fourth century B.C.), during which a transition was effected, from an aesthetic based on the ideal to one which turned towards the actual."

Unfortunately, space does not permit me to go into detail about more of the ancient Greek and Roman objects in my collection and the manner in which they were obtained. However, most of the major pieces in this portion of my collection are described and illustrated in the section of this book for which Jean Charbonneaux so graciously prepared his expert commentary.

At this point, it might be well for me to make a few observations based on my own experiences regarding the collecting of Greek and Roman antiquities.

To start with, the reader has doubtless noted that most of the items I've described were obtained from other private collections or, with a few exceptions, from dealers *outside* Greece or Italy. There are good reasons for this.

For many years, both Italy and Greece have enforced strict embargoes on the exportation of antiquities which were not already in private or dealers' hands at the time the laws were passed. The purpose of these laws is, of course, to insure that no additional art treasures are lost to the countries.

It is true that museums, universities and similar institutions will organize archaeological expeditions and projects and will frequently discover new troves of art and artifacts. However, even such activities are subject to stringent controls. The host country, Greece or Italy, may issue permits for archaeological projects and excavations, but seldom if ever to private groups or individuals. And the permits are granted solely with the proviso that the bulk—and usually the best—of any and all art or artifacts uncovered belong to the host country. The foreign archaeologists may take only a certain share of what they find back to their own countries, and then usually only if they are to be placed in university collections or public museums.

Ancient Greek and Roman art objects that were not already in private hands years ago are the property of the State or public museums. The days when a Lord Elgin could ship large quantities of ancient Greek marbles out of Greece are long past.

There are exceptions, of course. An Italian farmer excavating the foundations of a new barn might accidentally unearth a marble bust or a bronze statue. If he is sophisticated and unscrupulous enough, he will not report his find to the authorities, but will slip the object to some dealer no more scrupulous than himself. The dealer will, in turn, either offer it "under the counter" to some especially avid or particularly gullible collector, or will smuggle the object out of the country and sell it abroad.

To buy any object from such dubious sources is obviously risky. In the first place, the buyer is contravening, or at least conspiring to contravene the law, and is liable to penalties ranging from heavy fines to actual imprisonment. Then, the "rare object" he is buying may not be at all what it is represented to be. It could be a forgery, or even an object that has been stolen from a museum or private collection.

To all intents and purposes, the modern-day collector of ancient Greek and Roman art must confine himself to buying from one or another of two sources— well-established and highly reputable dealers or other collectors.

Even then, the wise collector will have the object he wishes to buy vetted by an outside expert, or even several independent authorities, if the purchase he is considering is important enough.

More than one otherwise prudent individual has been stung—and stung badly—by allowing himself to be talked into buying some mud-caked figurine which the seller purported to be a fourth-century B.C. Greek work or an example of second-century A.D. Roman art. Privately, even some established dealers will admit that they have been fooled. It must be noted, however, that reputable dealers will immediately and without question refund the full purchase price on any object that they sell and that later proves to be anything except what was represented.

The cost of having an independent authority expertize a work of art *before* he buys is the cheapest insurance any collector can obtain.

Notwithstanding all that I have said above, the beginning collector with only modest means at his disposal need not throw up his hands in despair at the thought of starting a collection of Greek and Roman antiquities. There are more of these around and available at reasonable prices than one might imagine. True, they are not the finest and the rarest and not of museum quality. However, they are still authentic, still beautiful and still very likely to increase in value as time goes on.

Besides, the astute collector starts small and gradually builds his collection. He can, by careful purchasing, buy items that he can later sell or perhaps even trade to obtain something of better quality and greater value.

Then — although the chances are not great, they are better than is generally supposed — there is always the possibility of making a real "find" in some flea market or junk shop. It does happen that the housewife who picks up a bargain marble bust at a rummage sale later discovers that she is the astounded owner of a rare piece worth thousands of dollars. More than one individual in recent years has purchased, say, a bronze statuette for a few dollars in a European flea market and had it prove to be a valuable piece.

One must never forget that objects of art frequently have a strange habit of traveling far and to strange places — witness the *Cottenham Relief*.

It is entirely possible that if I could comb through every cluttered attic in old New England towns, I might find many worthwhile works of fine art that have been gathering dust, unrecognized for what they are, for many decades. Many such works were brought home by the men who sailed the merchant vessels and clippers of the eighteenth and nineteenth centuries. According to references in the old diaries and the memoirs of such men, Greek and Roman marbles and bronzes — which in those days could often be picked up for practically nothing in Mediterranean seaports — were among the souvenirs they brought back to the United States.

What happened to all those treasures? Are not at least some of them lying in attics or cellars?

And this is only a single example of a possible source. I could, allowing my imagination a little rein, think of several others — and so, I'm sure, could any of my readers.

This brings us to a crux. In order to be a successful collector of any type or school of fine art, an individual must learn as much as he can about it before he starts collecting. He must be able to recognize what he is looking for, and be able to recognize at least the more patent counterfeits.

The studying involved pays many extra dividends. In learning about ancient Greek and Roman art, one cannot help but also learn about the civilizations and the people who produced the art. This will unquestionably serve to broaden the individual's intellectual horizons and, by increasing his knowledge and understanding of past civilizations, greatly aid him in knowing and understanding our own.

But then, all that is needed is a start — a beginning. Once an individual launches out as a collector, he will, in nine out of ten cases, become fascinated and enthralled. Even the most battered fragment of a statue, a headless terra-cotta figurine, or a cracked and dented bronze object will come alive, as fresh and as beautiful as the day when it was completed by its creator centuries ago.

And, when that happens, the collector can, at will, transport himself back in time and walk and talk with the great Greek philosophers, the emperors of ancient Rome, the people, great and small, of civilizations long dead, but which live again through the objects in his collection.

IV.

It is far from unusual for a collector to become involved in controversies over art. These may be as minor as a simple difference of opinion in regard to the exact year in which a particular canvas was painted. At the other end of the scale, he may become embroiled in—or stir up—a storm of dispute that falls little short of creating an international incident.

I know, for I once innocently found myself in the middle of just such a major imbroglio. The story of this incident goes back to 1928, when I attended the Rembrandt Exposition at the Boyman Museum in Rotterdam.

It would be utterly fatuous for me to add anything to the millions of words of praise which have been written and said about Rembrandt van Rijn and his work. The incomparable genius of this leading representative of the Dutch school of painting is too well known to require any comment from me.

Some forty of Rembrandt's paintings were assembled for display in the Boyman Museum—a fabulous *attroupement* of masterpieces that literally overwhelmed the eye, mind and emotions, and which no person could reasonably absorb in a single visit. One of the pictures shown was *Marten Looten,* Rembrandt's second commissioned portrait, which he executed in 1632, when he was twenty-six.

The more recent chronological history of the portrait was well known. In the early nineteenth century, it was acquired by Cardinal Fesch, uncle of the French Emperor Napoleon Bonaparte. Cardinal Fesch was then serving as the French Ambassador to the Vatican. After the Cardinal's death in 1845, *Marten Looten* was sold and became part of the English Coningham Collection. In 1849 it was purchased for 800 pounds by Sir George Lindsay Holford and added to his collection. In 1928, the same year as the Boyman exhibition, Anton W. W. Mensing, a wealthy and intensely patriotic Dutchman, bought the panel from Holford's descendants for $204,000. Although he added it to his own collection, Mensing bought it primarily so that *Marten Looten* would be repatriated to its native land.

Marten Looten was a painting that caught and held me. I was drawn back to it time and time again. To employ a much-abused, but in this instance entirely valid expression, Marten Looten appeared as though he would step from the "canvas"—actually a wood panel—and begin chatting with the spectators at any moment. The portrait made such an impression on me that long after I left Rotterdam I was haunted by it.

Ten years later, in 1938, I learned the great Mensing collection was being broken up. Among the items to be placed on sale was the *Portrait of Marten Looten.*

I was then in the United States and the press of business prevented me from going abroad to attend the sale personally. I immediately cabled the dealer through whom I normally made my art purchases in the Netherlands, telling him I was definitely interested in obtaining the *Marten Looten.* Aware that the aftermath of the Depression and the precariously unsettled conditions in Europe were keeping art prices at comparatively low levels, I knew the portrait could not possibly bring anywhere near what Mensing had paid for it in 1928. However, so great was my desire to own the painting, I authorized the dealer to bid up to $100,000 for it. This figure, taking into consideration the times and conditions which prevailed, was quite high. Also, following a practice entirely common in the art world, I instructed my dealer to keep my identity a secret and to say he was acting on behalf of an anonymous American.

The sale was duly held, the dealer acted to the letter of my instructions and, to my delight, succeeded in obtaining the *Marten Looten* for only $65,000!

At this point, a considerable amount of emphatic protest arose in the Netherlands, and particularly in Amsterdam. Segments of the Dutch press and public deplored the country's "loss" of the magnificent Rembrandt to an "unnamed American". Articles in Dutch newspapers and periodicals regretfully observed that a great national treasure would now go abroad, to a foreign owner and a foreign land. The loss was most keenly felt in Amsterdam, for Marten Looten, the subject of the portrait, had been a prominent citizen of Amsterdam in the seventeenth century.

Since the portrait had been in a private (the Mensing) collection and had been sold at a public auction, there were no legal or other restrictions on its purchase or its export. I knew that I had acquired the panel fairly and squarely and thought it best to ignore the criticisms that were being voiced and remain anonymous. I felt this course would tend to minimize the possibility of growing, or additional, controversy. It was the right decision. Before long, the Dutch aimed their criticisms at their own government, contending that it should have provided the funds necessary to top any and all foreign bids for the *Marten Looten* so that it could have been purchased for the Rijksmuseum. Nevertheless, a degree of regret lingered in Dutch art circles over the fact that the portrait had been acquired by an "unnamed American" and would therefore leave Amsterdam and Holland. Many years and World War II were to intervene before I would be able to erase the last traces of all such feelings in Holland.

In the meantime, the panel was shipped to me in New York, arriving there in January 1939. The New York World's Fair was scheduled to open on April 20 of that year. I contacted Fair officials and offered to loan the *Marten Looten* and some other important pieces in my collection for exhibit in the Fine Arts Pavilion. The offer was accepted and as a result I was able to share my joy in owning the masterpiece with millions of people.

Another decade passed. August 1949 found me once again in Rotterdam. The fascination that the *Marten Looten* held for me had never lessened. On the contrary, it had increased to the point where I avidly desired to learn all I could about the painting and the man portrayed. Also, I wanted to see if I could discover anything that might help solve the long-debated mystery of the letter that Marten Looten is shown holding in his left hand.

There had been countless theories about the letter and its significance and meaning. Before I bought the *Marten Looten,* a Dutch physician, a Dr. J. W. Kat, had announced that he'd deciphered the words scrawled on the letter by a "chemical-optical" process, the nature of which he steadfastly refused to divulge.

According to Dr. Kat, the letter depicted was from Rembrandt to Marten Looten himself and read as follows:

> Marten Looten XVII January 1632
> Lonely for me was Amsterdam; your company, friendship just gave me unforgettable peace created from an endless respect.
> (Signed) R. H. L.

The name "Marten Looten" and the date are perfectly legible in the painting. The "RHL"—Rembrandt's actual name was Rembrandt Harmensz Lugdunensis—is also legible. But the text, four lines in the painting, remains gibberish even under the strongest magnifying glass. Consequently, Dr. Kat's announcement had been greeted with howls of derision in the Netherlands and in world art circles. Innumerable other students of Rembrandt and his work had advanced other theories, none of which were widely accepted. It was my hope that, through patient research in Dutch archives, I might unearth some clue to solve the riddle.

Last, but far from least, my reason for visiting the Netherlands was to clear up whatever misunderstanding and resentment still remained as a result of my acquisition of the *Marten Looten* in 1938.

The art dealer who had acted for me at the sale graciously agreed to be my companion and act as my intermediary during my stay, using his considerable acquaintance and reputation to help open doors that might otherwise have been closed to me. When necessary, he also acted as my interpreter and translator, although this was seldom. The Dutch, like the Swiss, are usually bilingual or multilingual, speaking German and often English and French in addition to their own tongue. Although my own Dutch was limited to little more than guidebook phrases, I speak both German and French, therefore communication was not much of a problem.

Because I felt it would serve to provide me with a solid foundation on which to base my other efforts, I chose to tackle the identification of Marten Looten himself first. This required many days of searching through musty files, of shuffling through yellowed and fragile documents in the Rijksmuseum, town halls and elsewhere. Throughout it all, I carefully hid the fact that I was the unnamed American who had purchased the portrait. I posed, instead, as an American art journalist doing research for an article on Rembrandt.

Eventually, a fairly comprehensive description of Marten Looten and his life emerged from the hours of research and the masses of notes.

The Looten family had its origins in Aardenburg. Adherents of the Reform Movement, the family was forced to flee Aardenburg due to religious persecution in the 1500s. The Lootens went to Houndschoote.

In 1582 Spanish troops invaded Houndschoote and burned the city. The family sought refuge in Brugge. Evidently, the Lootens managed to salvage some of their wealth, for they were soon active and prospering in business again. It was in Brugge that Marten was born.

Some years later, the Lootens returned to Aardenburg, where they were now welcome. Dirck Looten became a brewer and eventually the mayor of the town. This peaceful, prosperous period was only a lull. The religious issue again forced the family to move, first to Aachen, then to Leiden.

Rembrandt's father, a well-to-do Leiden miller, became acquainted with the Looten family. Marten Looten, who was twenty years older than Rembrandt, moved to Amsterdam. In 1631 Rembrandt himself moved to that city. The most probable assumption is that the young artist — then twenty-five — contacted Marten Looten.

It is entirely likely that Marten Looten was impressed by the work of the budding genius and encouraged him. After all, Marten had become a successful grain merchant. However, being the youngest of seven children and only fractionally as successful as his older brother, Charles, who had amassed a considerable fortune in business, Marten suffered from what we would describe today as a marked inferiority complex.

Thus, it is not beyond the realm of possibility that he commissioned Rembrandt to paint his portrait to satisfy his own vanity. There is a substantiating element in the fact that, soon after the portrait was completed, Marten bought a large property consisting of a fine house and gardens for the then impressive sum of 4,600 guilders.

Old tax records showed that Marten Looten was well off. In 1631, he was taxed on the basis of a worth of 30,000 guilders. Thirteen years later, the tax authorities assessed his fortune at 71,339 guilders.

As for the disputed letter and Dr. Kat's deciphering of it, we turned up considerable evidence to indicate the good doctor and his optical-chemical system might have slipped a cog somewhere.

The tone of Dr. Kat's version of the letter is one of a man who felt sad and alone and who was humbly thanking a benefactor for having shown him kindness. But Rembrandt could hardly have been lonely in Amsterdam by January 1632. He had many friends and acquaintances in the city, among them some fairly wealthy and important persons. He was a rising young artist whose work was already attracting favorable attention (1632 was the same year in which he completed his world-famed *Anatomy Lesson of Dr. Tulp).* Nor, at that period in his career, was Rembrandt van Rijn's personality and temperament of a type to write a letter such as Dr. Kat purported it to be.

No. All indications pointed to the conclusion that the letter was nothing more than an accessory, a prop, with four lines of meaningless scrawlings, which the artist had his subject hold to give the portrait a more relaxed and realistic quality and to improve the composition of the picture. It was also a novel means whereby he could at once title, date and sign the panel. (Remember, the "Marten Looten", the date "XVII January 1632" and the initials "RHL" *are* legible.)

Further research revealed that the majority of authoritative opinion agreed with the conclusion I had reached.

Now I had achieved two of my goals. The long hours of research and study behind me, I felt that if Marten Looten ever *did* "step out of the canvas and begin to talk," I would be able to greet him and converse with him as though he were an old acquaintance. I also felt satisfied that I had solved the mystery of the disputed letter by determining that it was not, and never had been, a mystery at all.

Thus, I was ready to take on my final self-imposed task, making my peace with Dutch art circles.

On of the leading authorities on Rembrandt in the Netherlands was Professor Van Dillen, a member of the faculty at the University of the Hague. Coincidentally, he had also been one of the more outspoken critics of the sale of the *Marten Looten* to a "foreigner" and he deeply deplored the Netherlands' loss of the portrait.

I reasoned that if I could mollify Professor Van Dillen, prove to him that I was not an uncultured barbarian and that the display of the portrait in America had done, and would continue to do, immeasurable good by acquainting millions with the glories of Dutch art, the entire problem would be solved. I therefore asked my dealer friend to arrange an appointment for me with the professor.

"But don't tell him I'm the man who bought the *Marten Looten,*" I said. "Just say that I'm preparing an article on Rembrandt."

"Why on earth do you want to do that?" my friend demanded.

"Because I want him to judge me without prejudice, as an individual, before he learns that I own the portrait," I explained.

Some days later, my dealer friend and I were received by Professor and Mrs. Van Dillen in their apartment on the uppermost floor of a traditionally styled old Amsterdam house — narrow, picturesque and located along a canal.

We had been invited for tea. I chatted amiably with the professor. Before long, a bond of warmth sprang up between us. I found him to be a learned, but by no means pedantic expert, with an excellent sense of humor and a great deal of personal charm.

Professor Van Dillen asked me many questions about the United States. Implicit, though never openly expressed, was his surprise that an American could be conversant with the fine arts and especially that he could possess any but the most superficial knowledge about Rembrandt van Rijn and his life and works.

Finally, I gently began to steer the conversation around to the *Marten Looten*. I asked the scholarly professor several questions about the portrait and mentioned that I had read some of the articles he had written about it—which I had done during the course of my recent research.

Soon, Professor Van Dillen shrewdly realized that I was showing much more interest in the *Marten Looten* than I would if I were merely preparing a general article on Rembrandt.

"Tell me," he murmured quietly, "why are you so intensely interested in even the most minor details regarding the *Marten Looten*?"

"Because, sir, I am the 'unnamed American' who purchased it in 1938," I replied.

The professor was startled, and for a few moments he said nothing.

"I can understand how you felt about it, sir," I continued. "However, the *Marten Looten* was not lost to the Netherlands—for it, like every Rembrandt, will forever be Dutch. The portrait is in America, that is true. However, it is acting as a cultural ambassador of your country and its heritage."

I went on to describe where and how the painting had been exhibited, how it had been viewed by millions and would be viewed by millions more, for I was soon to donate the *Marten Looten* along with some other of the finest pieces in my collection to the Los Angeles County Museum.

The professor's face gradually softened and finally broke into a huge and sincere smile. I had won not only my goal, but a friend. When at last we parted the last of Professor Van Dillen's resentment against the unnamed American had vanished forever. I knew that within a very short time, all hostile feelings throughout Dutch art circles would also be permanently erased.

When I left Amsterdam soon afterward, I felt deeply content. I'd accomplished much. Few collectors are fortunate enough to become as intimately acquainted with their treasures as I had become with both *Marten Looten* and the master who had painted his portrait. I had satisfied myself regarding a controversy that had long raged over the letter which Marten Looten is shown holding in the painting. Above and beyond this, I had succeeded in ending a much greater controversy over the purchase and ownership of a great Dutch painting by an American. In that, I felt I had really accomplished something worthwhile, helping in at least some small degree to cement the bonds of cultural understanding and friendship between those who love and appreciate fine art in two countries, Holland and my own.

Excitement, romance, drama, a sense of accomplishment and even of triumph are all present in collecting. And I think this little story of the Rembrandt *Portrait of Marten Looten* serves well to prove the point.

V.

The focal point in my collection of paintings has been the Renaissance period. On the other hand, I have never pretended or aspired to assemble a completely homogeneous collection, to "super-specialize" by acquiring works which date from and solely represent that particular period.

I have already described some of the more outstanding of my digressions; it might be advisable for me to further explain and clarify my philosophy and approach.

It would not surprise me at all if the ultra-purists characterized my collection of paintings as one that lacks any clearly defined unity. Let the ultra-purists think what they may. Like the ancient eclectic philosophers who selected such doctrines as pleased them in every school, I seek to acquire such paintings as please me in the sense that I feel they possess true and permanent artistic merit and value.

I have often been asked why I've made no forays into collecting the ultra-moderns, or have not supported contemporary art. Those who ask me are always somewhat taken back by my reply—which is another question.

"Why don't the avid collectors of contemporary art buy Titians or Tintorettos?"

I collect paintings that please my taste, and I believe that the collection on display at the Getty Museum is better for the fact that the items in it were selected carefully from examples of the schools and periods I know, understand and appreciate most.

However, although my tastes lie essentially in certain directions, I am grateful to say they have not atrophied. I think my tastes have remained sufficiently pliant to recognize and adapt themselves within reasonable limits to the merits and potentials present in other periods and schools.

Permit me, for the moment, to return to my ten paintings by the Spanish Impressionist Joaquin Sorolla y Bastida. By any ultra-purist's yardstick, these would appear to clash glaringly with, say, my examples of works from the Italian Renaissance or the Flemish school.

Sorolla y Bastida and Titian and Tintoretto or Rembrandt and Rubens?

To the pedant and doctrinaire, the combinations would be abominable in a collection. They would not imply eclecticism but anarchism. However, as far as I—and a great many other people who have seen and commented upon them—am concerned, the Sorollas perfectly suit the "Lanaii" Room of the Getty Ranch House-Museum in Los Angeles, where they are hung.

The room itself is large, light and airy. Its design, decor and furnishings are cleanly and simply modern. The Sorollas are naturally suited adjuncts to their surroundings.

Notwithstanding what I have written above, I often wonder why more people do not have the artistic imagination to grasp and understand the aesthetic impact of strong contrasts. For example, Sutton Place, where I spend a not inconsiderable portion of my time, is a manor house located near Guildford in Surrey, some thirty miles outside London. Dating from the first half of the sixteenth century, and built by Sir Richard Weston, one of King Henry VIII's courtiers, it is a magnificent, and some authorities claim the finest example extant of Tudor architecture.

The great old house has a long and thrilling history. Queen Elizabeth I stayed there for a time when she was a young girl. Richard Weston's son was beheaded by order of King Henry VIII for having allegedly committed adultery with Anne Boleyn, Henry VIII's second wife. Anne Boleyn was also beheaded by the King's command, and it is a centuries-old legend that her ghost haunts Sutton Place—particularly the "Red Room" (so called because of its predominantly red decor) which had been her bedroom during her visits to the manor.

Through the generations, Sutton Place collected its legends and traditions and finally became the country seat of the late Duke of Sutherland, from whom the property was purchased in 1960.

The principal reception rooms of the ancient mansion are huge. Many are lofty-ceilinged and richly paneled in oak, mahogany or pine. After Sutton Place was purchased, both the interior and exterior of the 72-room manor house were completely refurbished and restored.

The "Great Hall," which is 57 feet long and 25 feet wide with 31-foot-high ceilings is a perfect room in which to display Rubens' large ($92^1/_2$ by 72 inches) canvas of *Diana and Her Nymphs Departing for the Hunt,* which I obtained in 1961, and the $60^1/_2$- by $94^1/_2$-inch Snyders-Boeckhorst *The Pantry,* a canvas I acquired in 1960.

The "Long Gallery"—165 feet long and 22 feet wide and oak-paneled from floor to ceiling—is perfectly suited for hanging Brussels and Flemish tapestry panels, as is the 65-foot-long dining room. The library, 135 feet long and 22 feet wide with its velvet-covered walls, high ceiling and large expanse of window area, lends itself ideally as a "gallery" for large eighteenth-century portraits such as Pompeo Batoni's *Portrait of John Chetwynd, Earl of Shrewsbury and Talbot,* measuring $71^3/_4$ by 108 inches and Gainsborough's 86- by 61-inch *Portrait of Anne, Countess of Chesterfield.*

What I'm trying to emphasize is that the periods, styles and sizes of the works of art I've mentioned ideally suit the style of the house and the rooms in which they are displayed. They "fit in" perfectly.

However—and I return now to my argument about the aesthetic impact of strong contrast—Camille Pissaro's *La Briqueterie à Erangny* or the Gauguin landscape, though apparently completely out of character with the other paintings, provide refreshing contrast. Rather than being distracting, or detracting from each other, the works of the old masters and those of the Impressionists, if properly and tastefully placed, serve to mutually highlight each other.

Before I loaned the *Madonna of Loreto* to the National Gallery in London for temporary exhibition there, it hung on a wall of the principal bedroom at Sutton Place. On another wall of the same room also hung Pierre Auguste Renoir's *Deux Filles dans un Pré,* "Two Girls in a Field," as well as two other Renoirs, both small but exquisite examples of his work: *The Farm* (9 by 7 inches), and *Landscape, Midi-Southern France* ($12^1/_4$ by $7^1/_2$ inches).

The paintings proved to be entirely compatible companions. Raphael and Renoir can not only live together in friendly comfort in the same room, but each of the masters—although separated by centuries of time and vast differences in subjects, approaches and techniques—emphasizes the genius of the other and the merit and beauty of his work.

I'll be the first to grant that there are limits beyond which the employment of contrast should not, and cannot be carried. With all due respect to their creators, exponents and aficionados, I can't quite see hanging examples of Pop or Op art in the library alongside a Gainsborough or in the long gallery opposite an early sixteenth-century tapestry. The result would not be an aesthetically pleasing contrast, but a ludicrous clash to jar the viewer's aesthetic senses and sensibilities. The extremes would be too great; the effect would be disastrous.

This is in no way to imply that I condemn Pop or Op art. Although my own personal tastes do run in different directions, I would not argue that either school lacks artistic merit for those whose tastes and preferences have developed along those lines. It simply happens that mine have not, and as I've said repeatedly, I purchase objects of art that appeal to my personal taste and standards of artistic merit.

But, let us consider briefly the individual whose taste in home or office furnishings and decoration runs to the modern, even the severely modern. Try to imagine the effect—the impact—of one or two good classical or Renaissance pieces tastefully placed in a living room or office to at once offset and, at the same time, favorably emphasize the uncluttered simplicity of the remainder of the decor. Such additions not only increase the charm and effectiveness of the whole, but reflect imagination and an understanding of the advantageous use of contrast.

Conversely, a room furnished and decorated in a more traditional style can be aesthetically enhanced by the astute placement of a modern piece or two. Needless to say, taste and discernment are necessary to achieve the proper effect desired in either instance. These are individual qualities that can be, and most often are, acquired and refined. In my opinion, precious few people are born with them. I certainly am not among those few. My taste and discretion in art developed through the years, aided and nurtured by reading, visits to art galleries and museums and the advice and counsel of those much more knowledgeable and experienced than I.

I do not suppose that it was until 1938 that the sum of all these influences began to truly bear fruit. That was the year in which I acquired among other works, Pickenoy's *Portrait of a Woman;* Willem Kalf's *Still Life;* Rigaud's *Louis XIV,* which hung in the Tuileries Palace until the French Revolution; Gainsborough's *Portrait of James Christie;* the *Marten Looten;* and, of course, what later proved to be the original Raphael *Madonna of Loreto.*

I did very little buying during the war years. Almost all my time and efforts were channeled into personally directing the crash-program expansion and operation of the Spartan Aircraft Corporation, a subsidiary of Skelly Oil Company, a corporation in which I indirectly held the controlling interest. The story of my management of Spartan Aircraft has been told elsewhere and does not belong in this narrative. Suffice it to say that I took personal control at the request of Secretary of the Navy Frank Knox, who considered the tremendous expansion of Spartan and its efficient operation vital to the nation's war effort.

The production of airplanes and of subassemblies for thousands of fighters, bombers and other aircraft was far more important than art collecting. After V-J Day, I was immersed in reconverting my various companies to peacetime production.

Hence, it was not until a few years after the war that I was able to resume active collecting to any considerable degree. By 1951, business pressure had lessened sufficiently for me to get back into the swing. That year, the majority of my acquisitions were paintings, canvasses and panels of the Dutch and Flemish schools. Among them were Jacob Duck's panel, *The Rest of the Soldiers; Interior of the Church of St. Lawrence at Rotterdam,* a canvas by Anthonie de Lorme; Cornelis De Man's canvas, *The Family Meal;* Jacob Vrel's *Street of a Dutch Town,* a panel; and Joos Van Craesbeek's panel, *The Cardsharpers.*

Two years later, I was concentrating on Italian painters. The accretions to my collection during 1953 and 1954 include a sizeable number of paintings, some quite exceptional, by Italian masters. I list some below by year and, within each year by chronological order of the birthdates of the artists.

1953:
School of Paolo Uccello (1396—1475): *Battle Scene,* an odd-sized (17 1/2 by 65 inches) panel depicting the Siege of Troy.
Bartolomeo Veneto (c. 1480—1555): *Lady Playing a Lute,* panel.
Lorenzo Lotto (c. 1480—1556): *Portrait of a Jeweller,* canvas.
Bonifazio Veronese (1487—1553): *Portrait of a Woman,* canvas.
Gentileschi (Orazio Lomi) (1563—1639): *The Rest on the Flight to Egypt,* canvas.

1954:
Girolamo di Benvenuto (1470—1524): *Nativity,* panel.
Tintoretto (1518—1594): *Allegory of Vanity, Toilet of Venus,* and *Portrait of Doge Priuli,* canvasses.
Paolo Veronese (1528—1588): *Portrait of a Young Man,* canvas.

Some of the more significant additions to my collection in the years which followed are listed below, together with the year in which I obtained each particular work.

The Death of Dido, Rubens (1955); *Penitent St. Magdalen,* Titian; *The Cliffs of Pourville in the Morning,* Monet; *The Village of Essoyes,* Renoir; *Three Dancers in Pink,* Degas (the last four paintings were all acquired in 1956).

The Square Louis XV in Paris, Moreau the Elder (1957); *Portrait of Anne, Countess of Chesterfield,* Gainsborough; *Seaside Landscape,* Degas; *Landscape Near Rouen,* Gauguin (the last three paintings were all acquired in 1959).

In 1960, my purchases included the Snyders-Boeckhorst *The Pantry* and Bonnard's *Woman in the Nude.* The following year, I achieved something of a coup by obtaining Peter Paul Rubens' breathtakingly beautiful and luminescent canvas, *Diana and Her Nymphs Departing for the Hunt,* a famed masterpiece for which I paid a very large sum of money. The next year saw another happy triumph. I succeeded in obtaining another Rembrandt, *Saint Bartholomew,* which throughout its long and meticulously documented history was variously and erroneously known as *The Assassin, Man With a Knife* and *Portrait of Rembrandt's Cook.* I purchased this painting at Sotheby's, paying 190,000 pounds sterling, plus 6,000 pounds commission, or a total at current exchange rates of nearly $550,000. I derived immense and special pleasure from acquiring this canvas for two reasons.

First, the *Saint Bartholomew* has helped ease my nostalgic longing for the *Marten Looten,* which I'd donated to the Los Angeles County Museum several years earlier. Second, I was highly gratified by the reaction in Dutch art circles to my purchase of the *Saint Bartholomew.* This time, according to reports I received, there were expressions of satisfaction and approval that the painting had gone to someone who had genuine love and appreciation for the work of Rembrandt van Rijn. My interview with Professor Van Dillen in Amsterdam had paid rich rewards.

A recent (May, 1964) acquisition has been the *Self-Portrait* by Paolo Veronese (Paolo Caliari), which is on temporary loan to the National Gallery in London, along with the *Madonna of Loreto.* The *Self-Portrait* is in excellent company, for the National Gallery has hung it in a room that holds some of the choicest works of Veronese, Titian and Tintoretto.

According to data I have obtained, the Paolo Veronese had led a very interesting life, especially since the beginning of the nineteenth century, when it was well over 200 years old. In April 1802, according to the authoritative Italian book *Paolo Vero-*

nese, Sua Vita e Sue Opera ("Paolo Veronese, His Life and His Works"), the following occured (quoted in translation):

"In the month of April [1802] in Verona, the *Portrait of Paolo,* painted by himself, and belonging to the Countess Salvi-Pindmonte-Moscardi [sic], was sold to the Englishman, Lord Prijor [sic] for the price of 500 gold napoleons. ..."

The next mention of it is found shortly before the outbreak of World War II, when the 76- by 53-inch canvas was purchased from an English country home by a Dutch dealer who took it to Holland. During the war, it was "acquired" by Hitler's right-hand man and chief of the Nazi Luftwaffe, Hermann Goering, and it became part of Goering's collection.

After the war, it was brought to England, where it was sold at Sotheby's. For some unaccountable reason, it brought a paltry price, namely £ 90. It was purchased by a dealer who, according to what I've heard, sold it before long for around $ 1,250, still a very meager price.

The painting soon came into the possession of a famous international art dealer. After his death, I acquired the Paolo Veronese *Self-Portrait* from his heirs in a private sale. I paid a price that was many thousands of times greater than the sum it brought at Sotheby's, but even so, art authorities tell me I got a great bargain. The painting, they say, is worth much more than what I paid for it, and it is acknowledged to be one of the finest works of Paolo Veronese and executed entirely by his own hand.

Space limitations have made it utterly impossible for me to mention or to include descriptions and reproductions of every painting I have acquired over the years. I have touched on only a few of the more important, unusual or especially interesting items. As for the illustrations and additional descriptions that appear in this volume, I feel that the editors have chosen carefully and well, selecting examples that provide a truly representative sampling and reflect the scope, range and "feel" of the collection.

Once again, I'd like to pass on some of the pointers I've learned. Much of what I said earlier about antiquities holds with equal validity for paintings.

As a rule, paintings should only be purchased through reputable dealers or, obtained through private sources, only after consultation with a qualified expert. There is, of course, an exception to this rule when dealing with living artists. Individuals who collect the works of contemporary artists can often buy directly from them at their studios.

Much caution is needed in buying paintings, whether those of old masters or living moderns. There are many, all too many, wrongly attributed or totally spurious paintings about, as well as large numbers that have been stolen from their rightful owners. Such is the traffic in bogus or stolen paintings that Interpol, the international police organization, was reported in 1963 to be establishing a special branch for the express purpose of waging war against art thieves and forgers. Art thefts are frequently reported in the press. Thieves know that a ready and lucrative market exists for their readily transportable loot. Highly organized gangs specialize in this form of larceny — for example, the gang that, a few years ago, broke into a French Riviera restaurant famed for its spectacular collection of modern paintings and stole more then twenty canvasses worth a fortune. These included works by Braque, Bonnard, Picasso, Rouault, Modigliani, Miro, Buffet and Dufy.

Counterfeits? They are legion.

As recently as June 1965, Italian police smashed an art counterfeiting ring operating in Florence, which they said, had been operating for several years without being detected. The culprits had been producing (and selling) spurious paintings in wholesale lots — supposedly the work of such modern artists as De Chirico, Guttuso, De Pisis and many others. Indicative of the scale of the operation, the authorities seized no less than 150 bogus De Chiricos which the forgers had in their headquarters, ready for shipment.

So good was the counterfeiters' work, Italian authorities declared, that dealers and private collectors in Paris, Berlin, Stockholm, London and the United States had been completely duped. The police said that the forgers concentrated on counterfeiting modern artists whose high status was accepted, but whose works were not so thoroughly catalogued as those of the old masters. It was estimated that some thousands of fraudulent works had been produced and sold by this one ring alone in the last four or five years.

Old masters are forged, too, and offered to and purchased by the gullible who fail to take the simple precaution of having the painting examined by one or more experts. I say "one or more" not because I am suggesting an expert may not render an honest verdict, but because some forgeries are so good that it may require several highly qualified authorities on the particular period or painter to detect the revealing flaws.

It might well seem to the reader that, and no play on words intended, I am painting a very dark and discouraging picture for the tyro collector or the individual who would like to start a collection.

But there are good buys available, regardless of what period or school interests the collector, in every European country.

By no means does the individual wishing to start a collection need to go to Europe to do his or her shopping. There are many highly reputable and totally reliable art dealers in the United States. Naturally, their prices are likely to be somewhat higher than those prevailing for similar items in Europe. There are transportation, insurance and other costs which must be taken into consideration.

Nevertheless, the shrewd collector and careful shopper can still find paintings of merit at prices to fit his means in the United States. And, it must certainly be borne in mind that there have been, and are, a great many fine American artists whose works are as good and as highly regarded, level for level, as those produced by artists anywhere in the world.

The individual who wishes to start a collection should never overlook the potential of young "beginning" artists. If the collector has a basic understanding and feeling for paintings and has developed his tastes to any appreciable degree, the possibility of finding an artist who will eventually reach top rank is always present. The Braque which once sold for $15 and in 1959 brought $155,000, and innumerable similar cases that I or any other experienced collector could cite, are positive proof of this.

Here, I would like to interject a few reminders that might seem minor to some, to others self-evident and thus redundant, but that concern matters all too often overlooked. The first regards the framing of paintings. It is foolish to purchase a painting and then to provide it with a frame of inferior quality or one which does not suit the painting. Any painting which an individual feels is worth buying and having deserves to be framed properly. Artists and art dealers can and generally will give constructive suggestions, taking into consideration not only the character and characteristics of the painting but also those of the room in which it is to be hung. When necessary, they will usually be able to recommend competent, reliable picture framers.

Next, I would like to mention the display of paintings. Obviously, no hard and fast rules exist. Much—in fact, almost all—depends on the painting, the nature, size and decor of the room in which it is to be hung and, last but not least, the personal taste of the owner. However, a painting should be displayed to advantage, so that it can "show itself" at its best. There should be artistry in the hanging of pictures on a wall just as in the paintings themselves. And, of course, a painting should have proper lighting—lighting that enhances its beauty and, whenever possible, serves to further emphasize whatever effect the artist has tried to achieve.

Last, a word or two about the care and preservation of paintings. They should not be exposed to extremes of temperature or humidity or to direct sunlight. When they require cleaning or repair, these operations must be performed by qualified professionals. A painting cannot be cleaned properly or safely by even the most meticulous housewife. (I know of one painful and ultra-extreme incident in which a well-meaning housewife took a hanging, an oil painting on so-called "monk's cloth" worth $750, and ran it through her washer-spin-dryer because it was dusty and grimy!)

By the same token, the repair of a painting or even of a good picture frame is hardly a chore to be undertaken by even the handiest "Mr. Fixit" home repairman. Such tasks are for specialists and the amateur will at best only worsen the existing damage or defect, and at worst will cause irreparable harm and destroy not only the value but also the beauty of the painting.

These points covered, I would like to offer one final counsel. Whatever school or type of painting the collector chooses to collect, let the choice be his own, in accord with his own taste and preference. One of the greatest joys of collecting lies in the gratification an individual derives from obtaining an object that he wants and that satisfies his *own* tastes.

"Following the crowd," and collecting certain types of objects or certain schools of painting just because it is the "fashionable" thing to do or the fad of the moment provides no real and lasting satisfaction, offers no excitement and gives no joy.

Someone once criticized my collection to Sir Alec Martin of Christie's, arguing that I collected in unrelated categories, that my collection lacked the singleness of purpose and the concentration that he, the critic, felt should characterize a collection.

The critic concluded his tirade by disdainfully sneering: "Paul Getty buys only what *he* likes!"

Since Sir Alec Martin's reply and comment have been widely published in a book written by Ralph Hewins, I feel that I can quote it here without compunction and without feeling that I am being unduly immodest in doing so.

"I don't hold it against him at all that his collections are an expression of the man," Sir Alec declared. "I'm rather fed up with these impersonal, 'complete' collections which are chosen by somebody for somebody else. The formation of his wonderful collection has been a public service."

No collector could hope for greater vindication of his collecting philosophy, or for higher praise of his collection.

VI.

On viewing the *Ardabil* carpet, James A. Whistler, the great American painter and etcher, confessed that he was awestruck and declared it to be "worth all the pictures ever painted".

The *Ardabil,* measuring 23 feet 11 inches by 13 feet 5 inches, was made in Persia during the first half of the sixteenth century. It must have taken many years to make and was completed in 1539—40. It is universally conceded to be the world's finest Persian carpet. The *Ardabil* and a less superb but still magnificent carpet of similar size and two exquisite, smaller prayer rugs were loomed for the most holy of all Persian religious shrines, the Mosque of Safi-ud-din.

Such was the beauty of the *Ardabil* that for more than 200 years the Moslem Persians stoutly maintained it was "too good for Christian eyes to gaze upon."

The *Ardabil* and its three lesser companions disappeared from the mosque early in the nineteenth century. One story holds they were looted by invading Russian troops; another version has them being sold at great price by the shrine's custodians.

In 1890 the four rugs came into the possession of an English art dealer named Robinson. The dealer, aware of the value of his treasures, proceeded cannily. He offered the lesser of the two large carpets to British authorities at a very high price, handily neglecting to mention that he also owned its superior companion piece. A campaign was conducted throughout the British Isles to raise, by popular subscription, the money Robinson demanded. The necessary sum was collected, the carpet duly purchased and presented to the Victoria and Albert Museum, where it is still displayed.

Eager for American dollars, Robinson now sold the remaining three pieces, the fabled *Ardabil* and the two prayer rugs, to tycoon Clarence Mackay. The *Ardabil* passed through three great collections in succession, Mackay, Yerkes and De la Marr.

When the De la Marr collection was put up for sale, Lord Duveen was aboard a transatlantic liner. He heard of the event in mid-ocean and dispatched a radiogram to his New York associates to buy the *Ardabil* at any price up to $250,000. Duveen had no intention of purchasing the carpet for resale; he wanted it for his personal collection.

Prices realized at the De la Marr auction proved extremely disappointing to all but the buyers. To his astonishment, Lord Duveen obtained the *Ardabil* for what was literally a bargain-basement figure — $57,000.

I first saw the *Ardabil* at an exhibition of Persian art in Paris. I fully shared the feeling of breathless awe it had inspired in James Whistler and countless others. The carpet, with its magnificent pattern, colors and sheen, was one of the most beautiful things I had ever seen in my life.

I immediately contacted Lord Duveen with a view to purchasing it. He flatly informed me the *Ardabil* was not for sale at any price. Knowing him personally, I realized he meant what he said and with great reluctance abandoned all hope of ever owning the treasure.

Then came the great war scare of 1938. Art prices in Europe plummeted as dealers and collectors panicked. Cash, particularly American cash, became a much sought-after commodity, for it seemed to offer the greatest security in the conflict everyone expected would begin momentarily.

Lord Duveen—it must be remembered he was then 69 and had only a year of life remaining—was not entirely immune to the contagion of fear and uncertainty. He sent me word that he had changed his mind about the *Ardabil.* While it was true that the bottom appeared to be falling out of just about everything, Lord Duveen still virtually made me a gift of the carpet, selling it to me for slightly less than $70,000. I also obtained one of the two small prayer rugs that had been in the Mosque of Safi-ud-din.

Not very long thereafter, the Princess Fawzia, eldest sister of Farouk, then King of Egypt, was to marry the Shah of Persia (Iran). I was approached by intermediaries acting for King Farouk who informed me that he wished to buy the carpet and give it to his sister and the Shah as a wedding present. The gift was intended as an adroit diplomatic gesture, for it would have effected the repatriation of the epitome of ancient Persian rug-weaving art to its native land. The price suggested to me was in excess of $250,000.

I turned down the offer as politely as possible. For a time, I used the *Ardabil* as a carpet in the penthouse apartment I was then occupying in New York City. The apartment had a room large enough for it, and the superb, glowing *Ardabil* caused more than a few of my visitors to gasp with almost reverential admiration when they saw it for the first time.

Later, the carpet was loaned for display to the Metropolitan Museum of Art in New York. After that, it was transferred to my home in southern California.

But, much as I reveled in the ownership of the *Ardabil,* I began to feel twinges of conscience about it. The Persians had averred it was "too good for Christian eyes to gaze upon." I, on the contrary, increasingly felt that the *Ardabil* was too good to be gazed upon only by the comparatively few people—Christian or otherwise—who visited my home. I therefore made a decision that, I must confess, was not entirely without pain, and donated the *Ardabil* carpet to the Los Angeles County Museum. I also donated another rare and exquisite example of sixteenth-century Persian rugs to the museum. This was the famous *Coronation Carpet,* so called because it had been borrowed from its owners for use in Westminster Abbey during the coronation of King Edward VII in 1902. I had purchased this Safavid Dynasty carpet at Christie's in 1930 for $31,500, a small fraction of its actual value.

In one of its quarterly bulletins, the Los Angeles County Museum described the *Ardabil* as "the million-dollar carpet." Independent experts have concurred in this estimate of its worth and feel that the value of the *Coronation Carpet* is almost as great.

Despite these gifts to the Los Angeles County Museum, I still retained a respectable collection of high-quality Persian rugs and carpets. Although none approached the *Ardabil* or the *Coronation Carpet* in value, many fine examples of Isfahans and Feraghans and Kermanshahs remained.

I have often been asked why I have devoted so much of my energy as a collector to acquiring carpets, tapestries and furniture. There are two reasons. First, I do not subscribe to the theory that only paintings, sculpture, ceramics and architecture qualify as major fine arts. To my way of thinking, a rug or carpet or a piece of furniture can be as beautiful, possess as much artistic merit, and reflect as much creative genius as a painting or a statue. Second, I firmly believe that beautiful paintings or sculptures should be displayed in surroundings of equal quality. Few men would dream of wearing a fifty-cent necktie with a $300 suit, yet all too many collectors are apparently content to have their first-rate paintings hang in a room filled with tenth-rate furniture that stands on a floor covered with a cheap machine-loomed carpet.

There is, I fear, a grave and widespread lack of understanding and appreciation for fine furniture and carpets even among people who consider themselves highly cultured and deeply interested in fine art. I have seen numerous demonstrations of this at the renowned Wallace collection in London. Crowds of visitors there will view the paintings on the walls of the rooms with rapt attention and sincere admiration, totally ignoring the glorious examples of furniture that are also on display.

Perhaps it is because the average person is conditioned to consider all furniture to be primarily utilitarian and only coincidentally decorative, and even then only *decorative,* not a form of art.

Whatever the basic cause or reason, it remains that rugs, carpets and furniture are seldom thought of as important art forms by most people. At best, they will think and talk in terms of antiques without consciously associating them with fine art. Hence, one constantly encounters such phrases as "collection of art and antiques," the obvious implication being that one has no relation to the other.

I must confess that I was one of that majority for quite a long time, viewing furniture and floor coverings casually and mainly as utilitarian objects. As long as they were comfortable, not unpleasing to the eye and harmoniously arranged, I paid them no special heed.

It wasn't until I found myself in need of a home base in New York City and leased an apartment there from Mrs. Frederick Guest that I suddenly became aware that furniture could have great artistic and aesthetic merit. A lady of infinite charm, great culture and impeccable taste, Mrs. Guest had furnished her apartment with an outstanding collection of eighteenth-century French and English furniture. One would have had to be a totally insensitive clod not to respond to the environment and to be impressed and influenced by it.

It wasn't that a spark was struck. It was rather that a blazing torch was applied, and my collector's urge flared high. I began to read and inquire, only to find that I was delving into a field that was highly complex and specialized, to say nothing of being strewn with perils and pitfalls for the tyro. Nonetheless, I refused to be dismayed or deterred. On the contrary, I went to the extreme of retaining several highly regarded art historians and authorities on fine furniture and carpets to give me cram courses on the techniques and tests for judging the authenticity and weighing the merits of such objects.

The more I learned, the more I was drawn to eighteenth-century French furniture.

The eighteenth century was the Golden Age of furniture, and France ruled supreme in its production. The Regency Period (1715—23) introduced the Rococo style, and interior decorations were made to match. For the first time since antiquity, the interiors of houses were designed for comfort and charm rather than for pomp and show.

The furniture of the Regency reflected a new style; straight lines were replaced by graceful curves, everything was less massive, less monumental. For example, the commode is an invention of the early eighteenth century and it soon became popular, for it contributed to the comfort and elegance of the new interiors.

Under Louis XV, who reigned from 1723—74, furniture became still more graceful, reflecting the feminine influence of Pompadour and Du Barry. Small secretaries with fall fronts, small boudoir tables and gueridons became popular. Rolltop desks are an innovation of this period, the classic example being the *Bureau du Roi* by

Oeben and Riesener in the Louvre. It has been said that this is the most valuable piece of French furniture to come down to us and that it would probably bring as much as $500,000 at auction today.

Louis XVI (1774—92) furniture is still feminine and delicate, but the taste of the times was classical and the curves of the Rococo period were replaced by straight lines.

Attempts to imitate great eighteenth-century furniture were made in the nineteenth and early twentieth centuries. The best imitations were produced by Dasson and Beurdeley in Paris between 1860 and 1890. Their imitations are difficult to distinguish from the genuine because they were made with the same materials and tools as the originals. There was no profit, however, in producing these almost perfect imitations. The standard of workmanship and material was so high that the imitations sometimes cost more than the originals would have brought at auction. The Wallace collection has a replica by Dasson of the famous *Bureau du Roi* by Oeben and Riesener. The replica was two years in the making and the out-of-pocket cost to Dasson was about 50,000 francs, or $10,000. This, at the time—the greater value of money and other factors considered—was not much less than the original would have brought if then placed on sale.

Beurdeley's commodes are top quality and are rarely recognized or identified as copies. On the other hand, common imitations of eighteenth-century furniture can generally be recognized at first glance by an expert. The wood is not old wood, the mounts are electroplated instead of mercury gilded, the chasing is shallow and mechanical and the whole thing simply doesn't "look right."

Soon after I'd decided to begin collecting French eighteenth-century furniture, I met Mitchell Samuels, the noted art expert and dealer associated with French & Company in New York City. Samuels had the complete confidence and respect of innumerable serious collectors and he quickly won mine. He graciously consented to give me his counsel and cooperation. I asked him to keep his highly trained and discerning eye open for any particularly good pieces which might become available.

Eventually, I had the good luck to assemble a collection of which I am proud. My acquisitions have come from many sources, some entirely unexpected. I should also mention that some of the purchases I made at sales were made under conditions that were distressing to the owners of the items, conditions over which neither they nor I had any control whatsoever. It has been my earnest hope in all such instances that I was of some benefit to those who had to sell because I was the highest bidder, paying the highest price anyone present at the sale was willing to pay. Otherwise, of course, I could not have been successful in purchasing the items. Luckily, instances such as these were few and far between. The overwhelming majority of my acquisitions were obtained under entirely normal circumstances.

Mitchell Samuels, with whom I became close personal friends, proved to be a uniquely talented and able buying agent. Through his efforts, the foundation of my collection was built. He assembled a nucleus of choice pieces around which I could, frequently with his advice and counsel, build further.

June 1938 proved an important turning point for my collection. Mortimer Schiff, financier son of the great banker Jacob Schiff, had formed a truly impressive collection of French eighteenth-century furniture, carpets and porcelains in his lifetime. On June 22, 1938, his collection was offered for sale in London. Prior to the sale, I went to the salesrooms with a friend, Leon Lacroix, who possessed considerable knowledge about eighteenth-century furniture. Together, we examined the items that were to be auctioned, and I made careful note of those I wished to buy.

Normally, in those days, I seldom attended such auctions or did my own bidding, preferring to have an agent act for me without disclosing my identity. This minimized the chance that I would be tagged as an active collector and consequently swamped with offers, catalogs, letters and cables, and personal visits from dealers from all over the world, which is the fate of all collectors who allow themselves to become known.

In this instance, I departed from my customary rule. I attended the sale and found the galleries jammed. It seemed that every English and French art dealer—plus a huge throng of other people—had also decided to attend the auction. My heart sank. With such an assemblage of potential buying power present, I believed I stood little chance of obtaining what I wanted, at least not at the prices I'd be willing to pay.

To my astonishment, most of the people proved to be viewers, not buyers. Bidding was sluggish, at times becalmed. Items placed on sale went for prices far below what might have been conservatively anticipated. Again, the grim tension and uncertainty that prevailed that year in Great Britain and Europe were having their effect.

I regained my confidence and entered into the bidding. Before the sale ended, I acquired several superb pieces that, when added to those I'd already obtained through Mitchell Samuels, formed a first-rate collection. And, what is more, I won out over competing buyers with bids which, if someone had suggested even a few days earlier would be successful, I would have considered impossible.

Among my purchases at the Schiff sale were the following:

A magnificent Savonnerie carpet, one of only two ever positively identified as having belonged to Louis XIV before 1667 (the other is in the Louvre).
The famed Molitor rolltop desk.
A Carlin Sèvres plaque side table.
A Tilliard damask sofa and chairs.
Two Chinese porcelain vases with French ormolu mounts.
Two Carlin Sèvres plaques gueridons.

That same year, also in London, I acquired from a dealer a writing table created by the mysterious all-time master of French eighteenth-century furniture who signed his works only with the initials: "BvRB." In recent years, he has been tentatively identified as Bernard van Riesenberg, a craftsman of Dutch origin who, for some unknown reason, preferred to remain anonymous save for his initials and who produced some of the greatest pieces of furniture ever made in France.

Incidentally, and throwing my narrative completely out of chronological kilter, I much later acquired another BvRB piece. This, the "Husband and Wife Desk" has been described by Pierre Verlet, Chief Keeper of the Department of Furniture and Objects of Art of the Louvre as "the most outstanding" example of this type of desk. While I'm at it, I might as well relate how I acquired this rare piece and thus confess to one of my colossal blunders as a collector.

In 1950, I happened to have lunch at White's in London with an old friend, the Duke of Argyll. Over coffee, he remarked that he had inherited "some eighteenth-century French furniture" and among the items was a desk he was willing to sell.

"If you're interested, you can see it," he told me, adding that it was in his ancestral castle located in northern Scotland.

He spoke in an extremely modest and offhand manner. As I did not relish the idea of making the trip, for it was the dead of winter, I decided to first consult a friend of mine who supposedly knew every piece of good eighteenth-century French furniture in the British Isles. I asked him if he thought the Duke had any pieces of museum quality among the items he had inherited. No, I was assured, there was nothing of particular importance. Hence, I did not make the trip to the Duke's castle in chilly northern Scotland. Instead, I left England soon thereafter for sunnier climes.

The reader can well imagine my chagrined reaction when, a few months later, my friend, the art expert, visited the duke in his ancestral home and identified the desk His Grace had so casually mentioned to me over lunch as being the magnificent BvRB "Husband and Wife Desk."

Clearly, I had missed a tremendous opportunity, for the duke—alerted to the value of the extremely rare and superb piece—had gotten in touch with several leading art dealers.

A year later, I learned that a prominent New York dealer had purchased the desk. I approached him and was able to buy the piece for my collection. It is worth every penny of the price I paid for it—but, the price was much, much steeper than it would have been had I been shrewder and acted swiftly and personally after my luncheon with the modest Duke of Argyll.—That anecdote sheepishly recounted, I shall return to the mainstream of my account.

After the infamous Nuremberg Laws were passed in Nazi Germany, the possessions of the Vienna branch of the Rothschild family were sequestered by the Hitlerian regime. Alfons, Louis, and somewhat later, Eugene Rothschild succeeded in getting away from the Nazis and managed to salvage a few pieces from their once immense and priceless collection of French eighteenth-century furniture. These were offered for sale at the greatly deflated prices characteristic of the period. For example, among them were two secretaires that, before the Depression, had been valued at $200,000 a piece, for they were exceptionally fine examples of the work of Carlin and Weisweiler. I purchased both from the widow of Alfons Rothschild (he'd died only a short time before the sale) for only $72,000, a price above which no other collector was then prepared to go.

Altogether and over the years, I have acquired many choice pieces from the collections of members of various branches—Vienna, Paris, London—of the Rothschild family. A few examples of these will suffice to indicate their type and quality:

Three Boucher Beauvais tapestries depicting the *Story of Psyche.*

A jewel or medal cabinet with a turquoise blue-bordered Sèvres plaque decorating its door.

An upright Louis XVI secretaire; two Carlin gueridon tables and a Carlin music stand; two Louis XV corner cupboards definitely identified as the work of another great French cabinetmaker, Jacques Dubois; a Jean-Henri Riesener writing table.

Among some of my other acquisitions from various sources through the years:

A Guerault table, the only other example comparable to which is in the Louvre; two Charles Cressent writing tables; a blue Sèvres vase with a bronze gilt base that had belonged to Marie Antoinette, and a commode by Gilles Joubert, the renowned *ébéniste* of Louis XV, made for "*Madame Louise de France*" and delivered by Joubert for use in her bedroom at Versailles.

Again, limited space prevents a complete listing here of all the items in the collection of French eighteenth-century furniture, almost all of which are now in the

J. Paul Getty Museum. I would, however, like to say a few additional words about the tapestries in the collection.

Altogether, I acquired several tapestries. Among them were four out of five of the Boucher Beauvais panels adapted from the legend of Psyche; several of his panels depicting the *Loves of the Gods;* and an extremely rare Boucher, a large panel into which two subjects of the *Loves of the Gods* are woven.

I also obtained some other fine examples of Boucher's works, along with Gobelins, sixteenth- and seventeenth-century Brussels and Flemish panels and other examples of this now all-but-lost art form.

Part of my collection of tapestries has been donated to the Los Angeles County Museum. Most of the remainder are now the property of the J. Paul Getty Museum.

The comments and suggestions I made and the warnings I sounded in foregoing chapters are all applicable to the collecting of furniture, carpets and tapestries.

Museum-quality examples are hard to come by—and, when placed on sale nowadays, are all too apt to command sky-high prices.

But, as with antiquities or paintings, the fantanstic bargain or the fabulous find are always possibilities. This is, perhaps, more true with regard to period furniture and carpets than with paintings and sculpture. For surely, there are store rooms, cellars, spare rooms and garages across the length and breadth of the United States that, unknown to their owners, contain unrecognized period pieces of considerable value that are considered only as castoffs by their proprietors. The day when a table or chair purchased in some squalid, jumbled back-alley junk shop turns out to be Regency or Chippendale is far from past.

There are also pieces of practically every period that, although not of museum quality or the work of famed artists and craftsmen, are still lovely and well worth collecting. Here, too, one can find prices extending across a wide range, and even the individual with a slender purse can obtain examples that have artistic merit.

On the other hand, imitations, "reproductions" and plain forgeries are as common in furniture as they are in other fields of art, and possibly even more so. There are also many instances in which carpets and tapestries are misrepresented. For example, it takes an expert to tell the difference between Beauvais and Aubusson. The former is far more valuable than the latter, and I'd guess that more than a few unwary buyers have been snared by unscrupulous sellers, paying Beauvais prices for Aubussons.

It is not overly difficult for the unethical dealer to convince the untrained lay buyer that a carpet or tapestry is much older than its actual age, or that a piece that contains sizeable areas of modern, imitative repair work is entirely original.

But, then, the problem of misrepresentation extends into all fields and forms of art, and laymen and tyro collectors are by no means the only ones liable to be victimized.

I recall one incident which serves as a textbook illustration of this. Among his many other attainments, Mitchell Samuels had long been recognized as being one of the world's great authorities on period wood-paneling. Some years ago, I was with him on a visit to an American museum, the name of which I shall mercifully omit.

During our tour of the museum, a tour conducted personally by its director (who shall also remain anonymous), we were taken to view a paneled room that, it seemed, was one of the institution's prouder exhibits.

The director at first beamed as he waited to hear Mitchell's verdict on the paneling. Then, after Samuels had run his highly trained eye over the walls for a minute or so without bursting out with words of praise, the director began to get a bit nervous.

Finally, Mitchell turned to face the museum director.
"What do they say it is?" Mitchell inquired innocently.
Now, the museum head was becoming distinctly apprehensive.
"George I paneling," he replied, trying, to maintain a confident air.
Mitchell cleared his throat.
"Um," he nodded and then suddenly asked the director a rather surprising question: "How old are you?"
"Why—I'm fifty-four," came the startled reply.
"Well, believe me—you're older than this paneling!" Samuels declared.
The director's reaction can be better imagined than described.
All collectors are well-advised to make all their purchases through reputable dealers and to call upon experts to verify the authenticity and value of all items they are interested in purchasing.
Not everyone can be fortunate enough to have as fine and knowledgeable an expert and friend as Mitchell Samuels as an adviser. But there are large numbers of men and women of unquestioned ability and integrity who can—and will—expertize items which are being offered for sale.
Incidentally, art historians at our colleges and universities form a body of experts that, for some strange reason, many collectors fail to draw upon. Perhaps it is because some people tend to be overawed by such titles as "professor" or "doctor" and are thus afraid to approach these authorities. Possibly, there are other people to whom it has never occurred that a college or university art historian can use his knowledge for purposes other than teaching, or writing weighty tomes.
Even those who collect on a very modest scale and fail to tap this great reservoir of expert academic knowledge are making a big mistake. Very often, a serious and costly blunder can be avoided or, conversely, a triumphant collector's coup can be insured by the simple expedient of contacting a member of the art faculty at the nearest college or university.
The professor or assistant professor or instructor, will be able to provide expert knowledge, or at the very least, refer the collector to a source from which it can be obtained. Doubtless, the faculty member will do the necessary expertizing on his own time, and it is entirely ethical, indeed customary, to pay him a reasonable fee for the service. The fee, quite naturally, will vary according to the amount of time and effort expended and the value of the object on which expert advice is needed.
No matter who the reputable, established expert consulted — professor, art historian or dealer — his advice and help will be of great advantage and value.
I repeat, using what I believe is the slogan of the nation's better business bureaus: "Before you invest, investigate."
This admonition is as valid for those who invest in fine art as it is for those who invest in stocks, business enterprises or in *any* thing, project or scheme. And for the collector who is, after all, an investor in fine art, the best, most expeditious and most reliable way to investigate is by seeking the advice and counsel of qualified art experts.
If an individual decides to collect furniture, carpets or tapestries, let the decisions regarding the types of items, and the particular periods that he wishes to collect be his own. As with collecting any type of art or, for that matter, collecting anything, whether stamps, coins or streetcar transfers, the individual should follow his own preferences and satisfy his own tastes.
It is thus that one savors the zest, and thrills to the joys of collecting!

GREEK AND ROMAN ANTIQUITIES

by

JEAN CHARBONNEAUX

[Member of the Institut de France]
[and Keeper of Antiquities in the Louvre, Paris]

SHELL ▸

Pentelic marble. Height: 8 ins. Width: 9 1/2 ins.

This object – unique of its kind – is a shell carved out of marble; most probably Hellenistic. It was discovered in Sicily and may be an acroterium from a temple dedicated to Venus.

◂ KORE

Bronze. Height: 4 3/4 ins.

Samos or Miletus; 6th Century B C

This indubitably Ionian figurine seems in its stiffness to belong to the tradition of the late archaic Samian bronzes, which are characterized by a somewhat frozen attitude.

Bibliography: For archaic bronzes of Samos cf. Jean CHARBONNEAUX, *Les Bronzes Grecs*, Paris, 1958, pp. 81–84.

The collection of antiquities in the J. Paul Getty Museum at Malibu, California is remarkable for its eclecticism. Generally speaking, collectors confine themselves to a period or a category of objects which is more or less strictly limited. The pieces which have recently been added to the Museum bring to mind those assembled by Rodin—with his interest in objects, regardless of the material of which they were made—at Meudon or at the Hôtel Biron. However, it is interesting that, at least among the antiquities, small objects and precious materials do not appear in this collection. We find, rather, a strong predilection for marbles. The predominant taste is for large sculpture. Greek and Etruscan archaic pieces are represented only by a few bronzes. J. P. Getty is obviously most interested in the great classical period; we can feel this interest in the choice of Roman marbles, although he does not confine himself to this period. It is not surprising, therefore, to find at Malibu several masterpieces from large dispersed English collections, notably three original Greek marbles from the Elgin Collection. I am convinced that the present owner's favourites are these three marbles, since every true lover of Greek art will naturally prefer an original to a Roman copy, even at its most impressive, such as the famous *Heracles* from the Lansdowne Collection.

◄ ARCHAIC KORE

Parian marble. Height: 28 ins.

Attic; early 5th Century B C

Fragment of a female figure draped in an Argivan double-pleated peplos, the right leg slightly forward. An almost identical statue is in the Athens Museum.

Collection: Elgin, Broom Hall (Scotland).

Bibliography: A. D. MICHAELIS, 'Ancient Marbles in Great Britain, Supplement 1', *The Journal of Hellenic Studies,* vol. V, London, 1884, p. 145, No. 2.

HEAD OF A HORSE ►

Bronze. Height: 4 3/4 ins. Width: 7 1/8 ins.

Attic (?); end of 5th Century B C

Furniture or chariot ornament?

This horse's head is an example of that 'subtle and nervous animal sculpture' mentioned by Charles Picard, who says that it was 'developed at the end of the Archaic period, particularly in Attica, but also elsewhere' around the middle of the 5th Century B C. (Charles Picard: *Manuel d'Archéologie grecque, La Sculpture II,* Paris, 1939, pp. 252–253.)

(Photo: Delmore E. Scott)

The preclassical period (the first half of the fifth century BC) is outstandingly represented by the Cottenham Relief, by a relief from Thasos from the Wix de Szolnay Collection and by a magnificent fragment of a figure wearing a peplos from the Elgin Collection. Each of these three sculptures is an example of a different style. The Cottenham Relief dates from the end of the sixth or beginning of the fifth century BC. It represents a young man leading his horse, one of the most characteristic Attic subjects of the period. There is, indeed, no more attractive subject in all Greek art. The horse and master are both thoroughbred; the subtlety of the young aristocrat's profile, the nervous elegance of his gesture, the beautiful animal raised and trained for racing, are emphasized by the sureness and sharpness of the outline. In this handsome fragment, all the grace of archaic Greek art is to be seen, but it is an Ionism distilled by the vigour of Attic genius on the eve of the Median Wars.

This relief has been singled out as one of the finest among the monuments to the soldiers who fell at the Battle of Marathon. The technical quality of the relief and its harmonious adaptation to the architectural whole merit a detailed analysis. Draughtsmanship, sculpture and architecture inspire in the spectator a more intense feeling than real life—no other art has so perfectly worked out the balance between these

three major arts as has archaic and classical Greek art. To begin with, we have mastery of the line, a line composed of long curves which are brought alive by subtle vibrations and which echo each other or cross with an infallible sureness. These outlines, which the eye can follow like an abstract design, enclose volumes created by variations in the modelling so discreet as to be almost imperceptible to the touch and which become evident only when seen in light and shadow. The projection of the relief is held within rigorous limits; only a very slight difference in thickness is necessary to bring out with extraordinary authority the superposition of two volumes—the right arm of the rider on the neck of his horse. A horizontal moulding is all that remains from the architectural frame, but this geometric fragment, at once rigid and supple, is enough to suggest to us the union between the relief and the architecture.

The Thasos relief takes us into another world. Here we can undoubtedly discern the influence of Athenian models, but the Ionian tradition to which Thasian art was still attached is stronger. The attitudes and the gestures of the nymphs who bring their offerings to the goddess still have an old-fashioned charm because they derive from the archaic convention twenty or thirty years after the end of the sixth century. The goddess herself appears to us seated and motionless, in full face like an Asiatic divinity. This relief belongs with those of Prytanis of Thasos in the Louvre, as the Cottenham *Rider* is related to the elegant athletes on the Attic vases of *circa* 500 BC and the reliefs from Themistocles' Wall in the Athens Museum.

The Elgin Torso is an example of Peloponesian art at its most robust. This figure, dressed in a rigidly-pleated peplos, belongs in its severity more to architecture than to sculpture. It is one of the oldest and most authentic examples of the Doric reaction which took place at the beginning of the fifth century, after the full development of the Ionian influence in statuary during the course of the sixth century BC. The difference between the Elgin Torso and the *Korai* of the Acropolis Museum in Athens is so marked as to make comment unnecessary. We should, however, note—despite the damage to the marble—the faithfulness of the traditional ceremonial gesture of the right hand lifting the drapery, evidenced here by a long, curved pleat.

CAT ▾

Bronze. Height: 12 3/8 ins.

Egypt; Saitic period (26th Dynasty, 663–525 B C)

The cat is sitting on its hind legs and wears a collar with an oudjat eye, a protective charm. This type of sculpture was offered up to Bastet, the cat-goddess, at the sanctuary of Bubastis during her feast days.

Bibliography: W. R. VALENTINER and P. WESCHER, *The J. Paul Getty Museum Guidebook*, p. 15. Similar statues are found in a number of museums; cf. Jacques VANDIER, *Guide sommaire du département des antiquités égyptiennes*, Musée du Louvre, Paris, 1948, p. 70.

◄ ZEUS

Bronze. Height: 6¾ ins.

End of Archaic period (c. 500 B C)

This statue resembles Etruscan bronzes of the same period through the stylisation of the beard and the folds in the tunic; but the resemblance to other typically Greek works such as the Zeus Lykaios of Athens or the Zeus at Olympia is much more striking. Said to have been found at Piombino (Tuscany). Purchased in London in 1955.

Bibliography: W. R. VALENTINER and P. WESCHER, *The J. Paul Getty Museum Guidebook,* Los Angeles, 1956, pp. 14–15. For comparison with the other bronzes mentioned cf. Winifried LAMB, *Greek and Roman Bronzes,* London, 1929, p. 88 and pl. 28 c, p. 94 and pl. 26 c.

(Photo Delmore E. Scott)

These three Greek marbles are the rarest pieces in the Getty Collection. However, the fourth century is represented by several remarkable originals and replicas of excellent quality.

Special mention should be made of the very beautiful bronze statuette of a young man holding a ram's head in his right hand. There is some question as to whether this is a remarkable replica from the Roman period or an original Greek bronze. Despite the fact that the missing left arm must have been cast separately (for that matter common practice during the Greek period, even for small pieces), I am inclined to believe it original. What is certain is that the form and modelling approached the Polycletian style. Pliny attributes to Naucides, the collaborator and perhaps the brother of the great sculptor of Argos, a *Man Sacrificing a Ram* who has been identified with the legendary hero Phrixos, who sacrificed the ram with the golden fleece to Zeus. It is quite probable that the statuette is a smaller copy of the *Phrixos* of Naucides, so that in addition to its fine quality it is of value in so far as it provides first-hand evidence of the style of this sculptor.

This discus-thrower or, more precisely, *Discophorus,* seen carrying the discus, his right foot forward, in position to throw, is generally attributed to Naucides on the authority of Pliny the Elder. In this statue, which dates from the beginning of the fourth century and which is known to us in several copies, we see the sudden outcropping of realism. The Polycletian attitude is modified, the movement of the muscles disrupts their ideal formulation, the disordered hair seems damp with sweat. One might hazard that here an apparently obedient disciple had shaken off his master's yoke in order to follow a completely different path. If, as we suppose, the statuette is really a faithful reproduction of the Phrixos of Naucides, this supposition takes on considerable historical interest. The general outline of the body, at least when seen from the front, is clearly based on the Polycletian model, as is the pose, with the left foot drawn back, the shoulder and head bent with the weight of the body. This is an example of the crossed rhythms perfected by Polycletus. But

(continued page 60)

◂ THE COTTENHAM BAS-RELIEF

c. 500 B C *Pentelic marble. Height: 11 ins. Length: 12 ins.*

This bas-relief, of which only this top left-hand portion has survived, represents a young man leading a horse by the bridle. Following the archaic tradition, the young man's head is shown in profile and his body in front view. Found by a workman at Cottenham, Cambridgeshire in 1911. The antiquarian Roger Gale (1672–1744) occupied a manor house at Cottenham in 1728, and it is supposed that this bas-relief may have belonged to him.

Exhibition: Burlington House, 1946 (No. 45).

Bibliography: Arthur Bernhard COOK 'A pre-Persic Relief from Cottenham', *The Journal of Hellenic Studies* vol. XXX–VII, part. 1, London, 1917, pp. 116–125; Charles PICARD, *La Sculpture antique*, vol. 1, Paris, 1923, p. 355; CHITTENDEN and Ch. SELTMAN 'Greek Art', *Catalogue of Burlington House Exhibition*, 1946, No. 45.

◂ KORE

Bronze. Height: 4 ins.

Etruscan (?), c. 500 B C

Small figurine of a woman with a pomegranate in her right hand; her left arm hangs down the side of her body and the hand catches at a fold of her garment. Paul Wescher has pointed out that the cutting of the garment is typically Etruscan, but since archaic Etruscan art is often so close stylistically to that of Greek artists who had settled in Southern Italy, it is sometimes difficult to distinguish between them. In this case, one might add that the placing of the left arm is common in Etruscan bronzes, and it can be seen in prototype in two decidedly earlier statuettes in the Louvre (early 5th Century B C) which are reproduced by Raymond Bloch in *L'art et la civilisation étrusques,* Paris, 1955, pl. 13 and 14.

Bibliography: P. WESCHER, 'New Acquisitions 1956–1957', *Bulletin of the J. Paul Getty Museum,* vol. 1, Malibu, p. 16, fig. 7 c.

THASIAN BAS-RELIEF ▸

Marble. Height: 14 1/8 ins. Length: 25 1/2 ins.

Thasos; Early 5th Century B C

Two women in profile carrying offerings (the first holds a dove) advance towards a square niche in which is seated a goddess (Aphrodite or Cybele) shown full face. The women are related to the three Nymphs of the Homage to Apollo in the Louvre (Salle du Parthénon), another Thasian bas-relief. Found on Thasos in 1913.

Collection: Wix de Szolnay, Vienna (Austria).

Bibliography: Charles PICARD, *Manuel d'Archéologie grecque, La Sculpture,* Paris, 1939, p. 87, fig. 40. P. WESCHER, 'New Acquisitions', *Bulletin of the J. Paul Getty Museum,* vol. 1; pp. 3–7, fig. 2 and 3.

◄ DOUBLE HERMES

Marble. Height: 6½ ins.

Ionian; Early 5th Century B C

This remarkable Ionian sculpture dates from the first half of the 5th Century B C and probably comes from Northern Greece. It is a two-sided Hermes, one representing Hermes, of which there remains only an ear and traces of a face, the other, in perfect condition, Persephone.

Purchased in Paris in 1958 (Koutoulakis).
Bibliography: 'New Acquisitions', *Bulletin of the J. Paul Getty Museum*, No. 2, 1959.

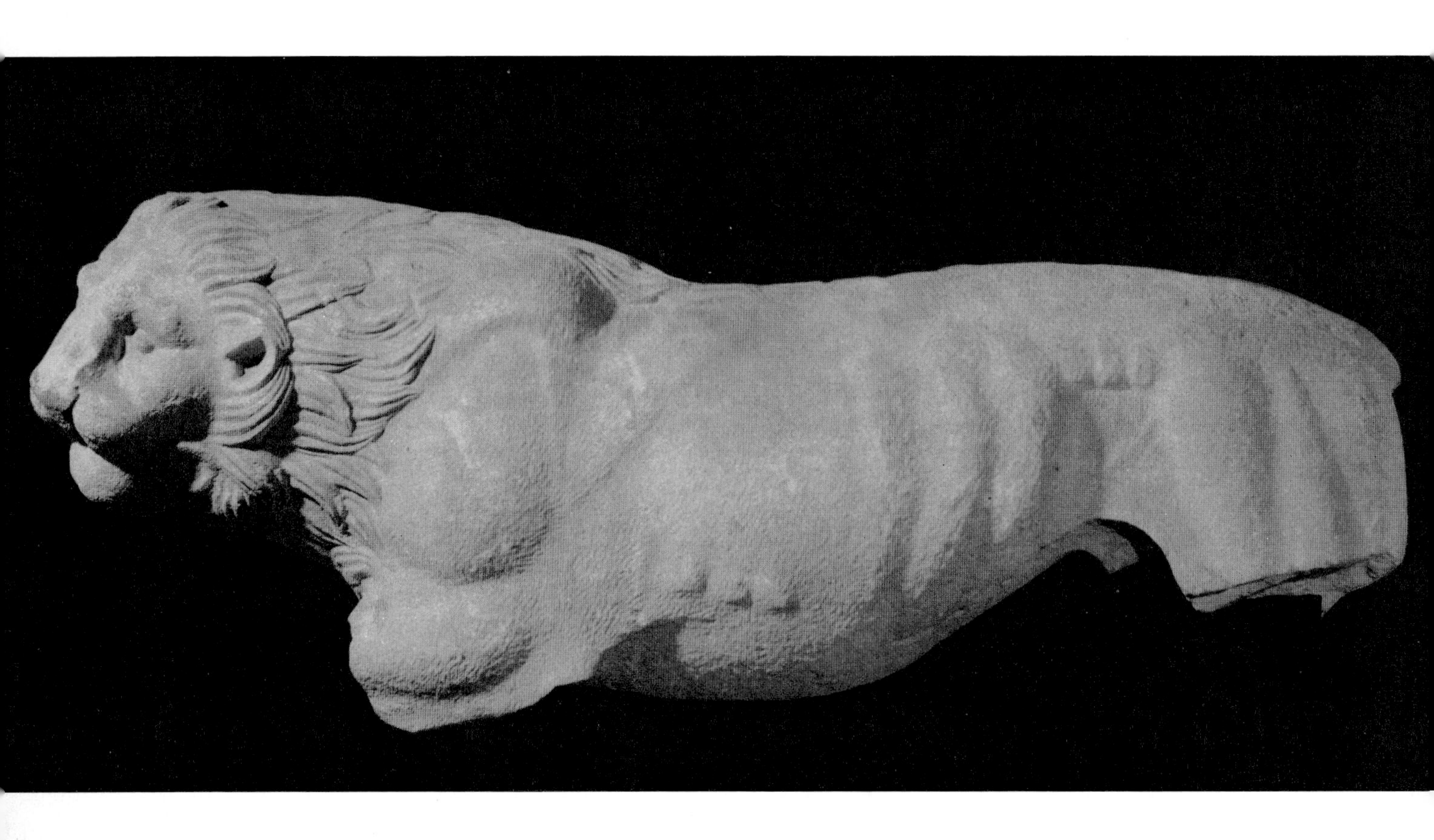

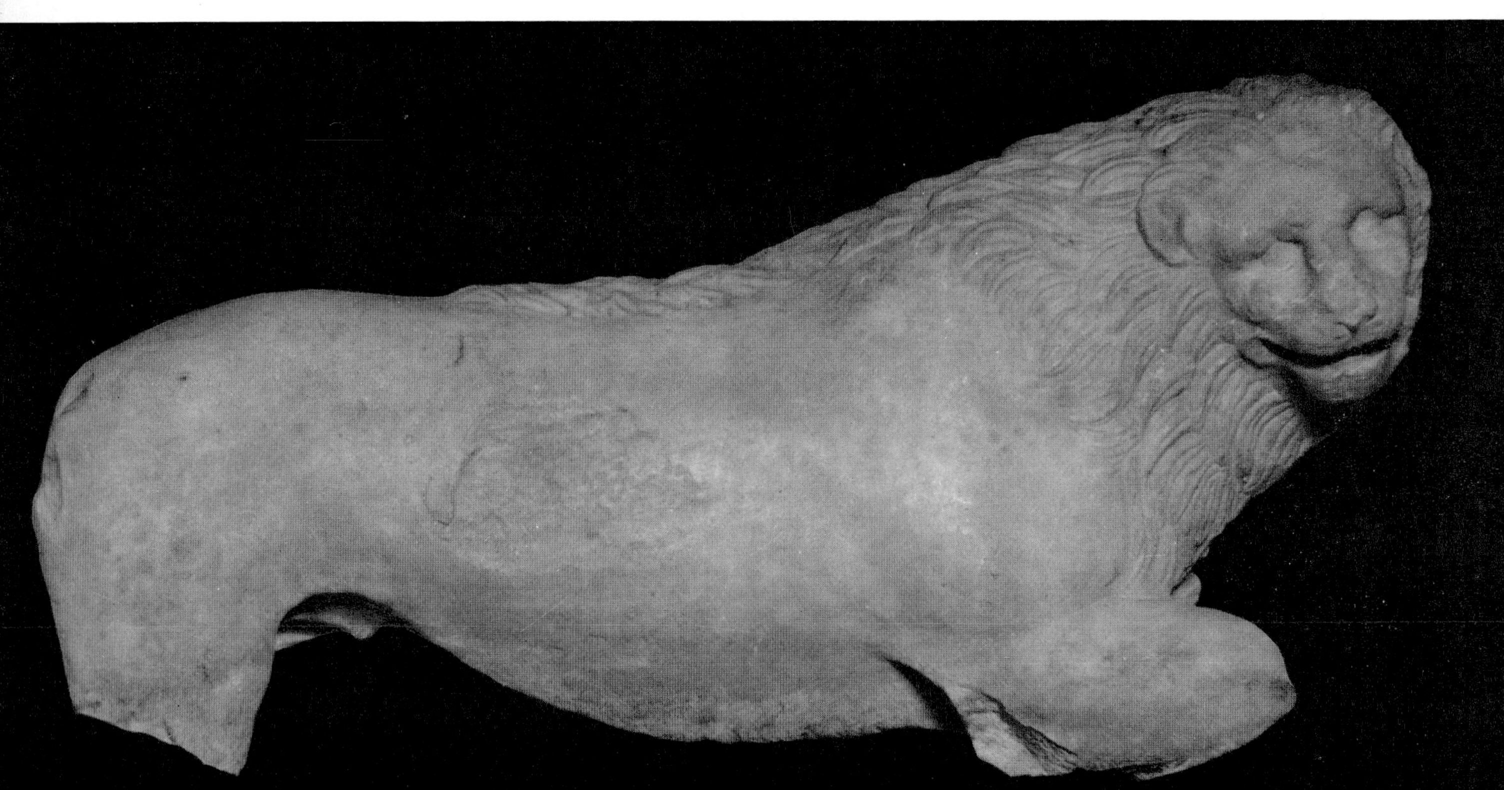

◄ LION

Pentelic marble. Height: 14¾ ins. Width: 8 ins. Length: 36¼ ins.

Attic; 4th Century B C

The crouching position, the almost straight back, the front paws turned in and the back paws on a vertical line are all indications that this was one of those funerary lions placed on private tombs. The funerary lion was a protective symbol. Similar statues are in the Metropolitan Museum (late 5th Century B C) and the British Museum, the latter a fragment from the Monument of the Nereids at Xanthos (same period).

Bibliography: H. STOTHART, 'Two Attic Funerary Lions of the IVth century', *Bulletin of the J. Paul Getty Museum,* vol. 1, pp. 18–20, fig. 8. cf. M. COLLIGNON, *Les statues funéraires,* Paris, p. 227, fig. 147.

▲ HORSE

Bronze. Height: 4 ins. Length: 3¾ ins. without tail, 4 ins. with tail.

Attic; 4th Century B C (?)

Few examples of this kind of statuette survive intact. The present example, of great elegance, is a portrait of a horse done from life. The mane is braided, the eyes inlaid with silver. The tail, treated in a different style from the mane, may (according to Jean Charbonneaux) indicate some eclectic neo-Attic style. A hole in the animal's back suggests that it originally had a rider.

Bibliography: P. WESCHER, 'New Acquisitions 1956–1957', *Bulletin of the J. Paul Getty Museum,* vol. 1, pp. 16–17.

◄ LION

Parian marble. Height: 17 ins. Width: 7½ ins. Length: 34½ ins.

Attic; 4th Century B C

Stylistically close to the preceding lion, but the work of another artist. There is no indication, however, that they formed part of a single group.

Bibliography: See above.

◄ FUNERARY STELE OF THEOGENIS, NIKODEMOS AND NIKOMACHE

Marble. Height: 43¼ ins. Length: 36 ins.

4th Century B C

A rectangular bas-relief framed in a manner which had become classic by the end of the 5th Century B C; the two side columns supporting an architrave and an equally narrow pediment resemble the structure of a small temple. Nikodemos, the central, bearded figure, with naked torso, his right arm bent across the lower part of his body, faces the spectator. On either side of him are two female figures: on the right Nikomache, draped and seated; Theogenis on the left, standing. They face each other in profile and hold hands.

Collection: Elgin.

Bibliography: A. D. MICHAELIS, 'Ancient Marbles in Great Britain, Supplement 1' *The Journal of Hellenic Studies,* vol. V, pp. 150–151, No. II.

FEMALE HEAD ►

Marble. Height: 12⅜ ins.

Ionian (?); 4th or 3rd Century B C

This head, damaged from the nose to the chin, seems to come from a funerary monument. The himation covers the top of the head and the hair at the back. According to Paul Wescher, the treatment of the eyes, and facial expression suggest an Ionian figure from Asia-Minor.

Bibliography: P. WESCHER, 'New Acquisitions 1956–1957', *Bulletin of the J. Paul Getty Museum,* vol. 1, p. 10.

PHRIXOS ►

Bronze. Height: 6½ ins.

Beginning of the 4th Century BC

This small statuette, of which the left arm – cast separately – is missing, is a perfect masterpiece of the Polycletian style. It has often been called a Hermes, but more likely represents Phrixos. In its right hand the figure holds a ram's head, symbol of the animal with the golden fleece sent by Zeus, which enabled Phrixos to reach Colchis before it was disputed by the Argonauts.

Collection: Julius Bühler, Munich.

Exhibition: Louvre Museum (Rotonde d'Apollon) in 1960.

Bibliography: Heinrich BULLE 'Eine bronzestatuette polykletischen Stils', *Münchener Jahrbuch der bildenden Kunst,* Band I, 1906, pp. 36–42.

◄ BUST OF A YOUNG WOMAN

Marble. Height: 13 ins.

Attic; 4th Century BC

Bust of a young woman or girl with a 'slice of melon' hairstyle; of outstanding artistic quality. According to J. Charbonneaux, 'This head would have been set on top of a draped body; this technique was common in Greece from classical times. Stylistically attributable to the studio of Praxiteles, it is one of the finest known examples of the refined Attic style of the second half of the 4th Century BC.'

Bibliography: W. R. VALENTINER and P. WESCHER, *The J. Paul Getty Museum Guidebook,* p. 13. P. WESCHER, 'New Acquisitions 1956–1957', *Bulletin of the J. Paul Getty Museum,* vol. 1, p. 8.

if we examine the pose, outline and gesture more carefully, we see certain significant differences which indicate a new conception of statuary. The exceptional precision with which the muscles are sculpted brings out some revealing details: we notice particularly the horizontal depression which crosses the white line between the clavicle and the pectorals; and this white line, more flowing and more disposed towards the leg carrying the weight of the body, harmonizes with the boldly accented hips. Views from the back and from the sides confirm these first observations; the oblique movement of the dorsal muscles breaks the ideal rectangular schema and follows the movement of the right arm, which thus takes on its full significance and indicates a revolutionary innovation. In fact, in the statuary of the fifth century the gesture is abstract and purely symbolic. The Parthenon Athena and the Olympian Zeus of Phidias, both holding out to the faithful a statue of Victory in their right hand, and similarly the Diadumenus of Polycletus knotting a headband — the sign of his success — around his forehead, are each fulfilling a ritual act which symbolizes their powers in the divine order or their qualities in the human order. Neither their expressions nor their attitudes are directly connected with the actions they perform, actions whose universal value stems directly from their timelessness. On the other hand, while keeping an harmonious balance of pose, the entire body of the Phrixos of Naucides takes part in an action whose immediate and concrete reality is emphasized by the eyes, concentrated on the object he holds in his right hand. Even if we still find it difficult to connect the Phrixos to the Discophorus, both of which Pliny

◂ 'MYTTION'

Pentelic marble. Height: 28 ins. Width: 9 1/2 ins.

4th Century B C

Unframed funerary stele topped by an faintly incised upright triangle. The subject, executed in low relief, fills the central section: a girl wearing a chiton, covered with a short cloak of a type unusual in Greece, holds a bird in her left hand; her right arm hangs down beside her body. The name 'Myttion' is painted below the relief.

Collection: Elgin.

Bibliography: A. D. MICHAELIS, 'Ancient Marbles in Great Britain, Supplement I', *Journal of Hellenic Studies*, vol. V, p. 148, No. 36.

HEAD OF A WOMAN ▸

Pentelic marble. Height: 8 1/2 ins.

Attic; 4th Century B C

This head is remarkable for its depth of expression and delicacy of feature, qualities which are undoubtedly Attic. The cecryphal may indicate that this is a servant, such as one finds on many tombs like the Hegesian Stele 5 (National Museum of Athens). This high relief sculpture has been dated by C. C. Vermeule around 375–350 B C.

Bibliography: P. WESCHER, 'New Acquisitions 1956–1957', *Bulletin of the J. Paul Getty Museum*, vol. 1, pp. 8–9. cf. H. DIEPOLDER, *Die Attischen Grabreliefs*, Berlin, 1931, pl. 37 and 41.

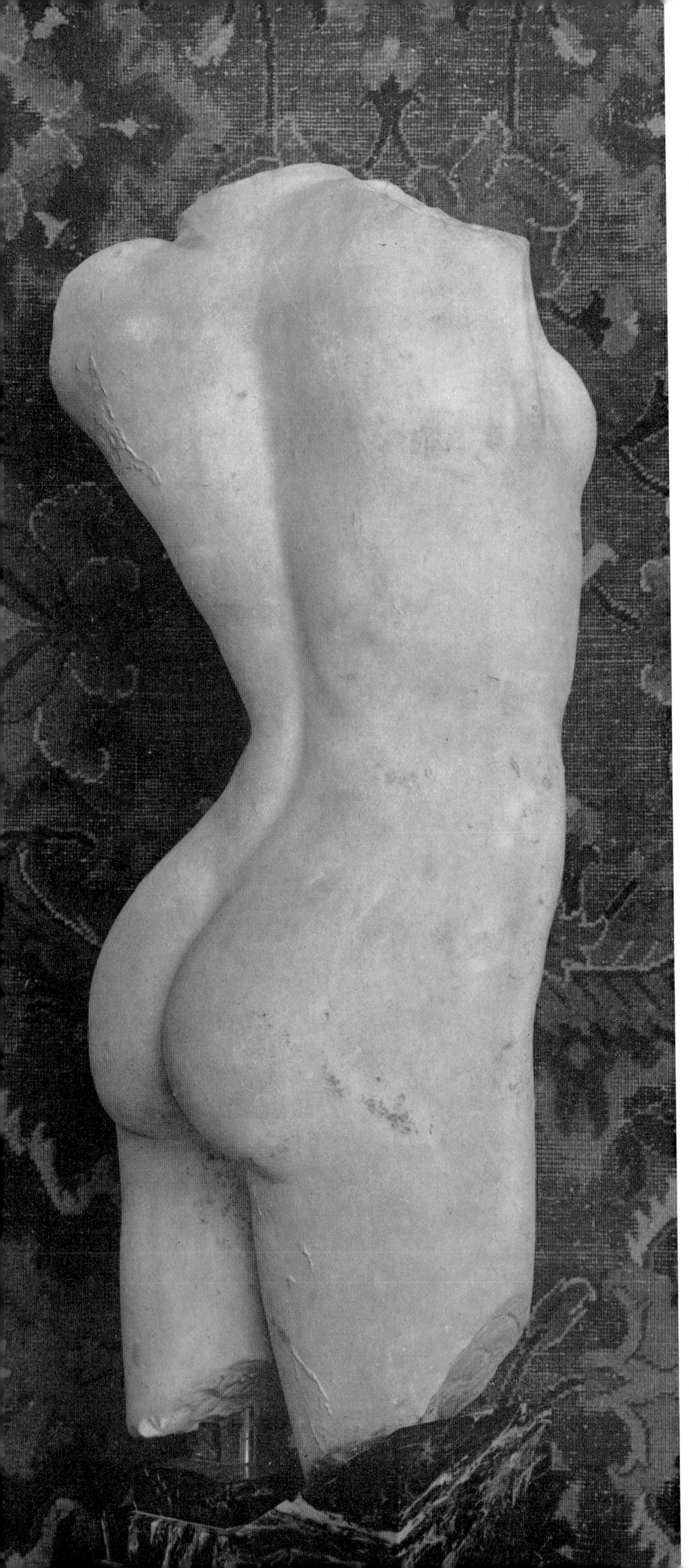

attributes to the same sculptor, we cannot doubt that the statuette in the Getty Collection occupies an essential place in the history of this important period, during which a transition was effected from an aesthetic based on the ideal to one which turned towards the actual.

We return to the Elgin Collection with two fourth-century funerary *stele*, one Attic and the other from Northern Greece. The former is a good example of the funerary sculpture of the middle of the fourth century, being treated in a broad style; the rounded volumes and the figures disposed in a semi-circle being characteristic of those reliefs in which the figures were detached from their architectural surroundings in an attempt to suggest an effect of space. The second *stele* is of a much rarer type and belongs to the Ionian tradition of the fifth century. The sobriety of the draughtsmanship succeeds in expressing the movement of the body within the tunic by means of a few curved folds which are incised rather than modelled. The gracefulness of attitude and gesture is emphasized by the strange rigid vest of leather or felt which confirms the Nordic origin of this charming relief. These two *stele* allow for a comparison which is the more instructive in that they are not very far apart in time. On the one hand, there is a fidelity to the purest bas-relief technique, which respects the tradition of the figure being slightly in relief on a plane parallel with the background and spreads the figure across the surface so that it achieves the maximum vivacity and decorative effect. On the other hand, under the influence of the monumental sculpture of the *metopes* and the pediments – and probably under the influence of the painters of this period – we

(continued page 68)

◄ TORSO OF VENUS

Marble. Height: 28 3/8 ins.

Italy; 2nd Century B C

This almost life-size torso is said to have been found in the sea at Antium (present-day Anzio) near the Villa of Nero. A Hellenistic work, it is known as 'Venus with Mirror'.

Purchased from the Barsanti Galleries, Rome 1939.

APHRODITE ►

Bronze. Height: 11 1/4 ins.

Syria; Hellenistic period

Naked and wearing a diadem, the goddess originally held a mirror in her left hand. Her right hand is raised to breast level. Her diadem is made of dwarf palm leaves, a typical decorative motif in Syrian Hellenistic works.

Bibliography: P. WESCHER, 'New Acquisitions 1956–1957', *Bulletin of the J. Paul Getty Museum*, vol. 1, p. 15. cf. DE RIDDER, *Catalogue de la collection de Clerq*, Paris, vol. III.

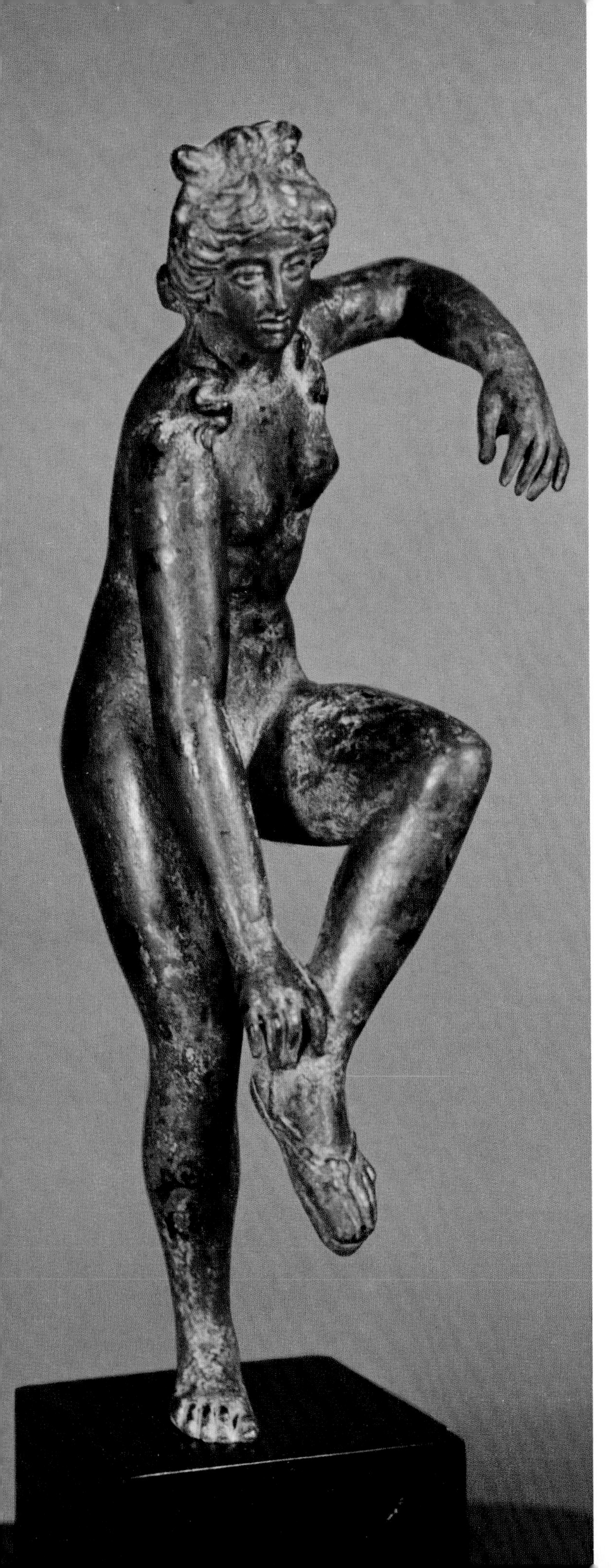

HEAD OF AN EPHEBE ►

Marble. Height: 12¼ ins.

The origin of this head is not known. According to Jean Charbonneaux it can be dated from the 2nd century BC.

Purchased in Paris (Koutoulakis).

◄ APHRODITE WITH A SANDAL

Bronze. Height: 8 ins.

Alexandria; 3rd Century BC

The unveiled Aphrodite at her toilette was one of the favourite themes of Hellenistic statuary (M. Bieber cites more than 70 examples, 39 of which are in bronze). Many stages of this subject are represented, but according to J. Charbonneaux 'one of those most frequently reproduced in small bronze statuettes' is that shown here, that is to say the goddess untying her sandal before her ritual bath.

Bibliography: On this subject, cf. J. CHARBONNEAUX, *Les bronzes grecs*, Paris, 1958, p. 101; M. BIEBER reproduces in *The sculptures of the Hellenistic Age,* New York, 1955, on plate 606 an almost identical example from the Naples Museum.

CROUCHING VENUS ▸

Terracotta. Height: $8^{3}/_{4}$ ins.

2nd Century BC

A Hellenistic statuette representing Venus, apparently a replica of the lost work of Diodalses, like the preceding marble (see p. 38).

◂ TANAGRA

Terracotta. Height: $10^{1}/_{2}$ ins.

Boeotia; 3rd Century BC

A standing woman wearing a cloak and tunic; her head uncovered, hair waved and parted in the middle and pulled back. Her bare left arm rests on her hip. Discovered on the shores of Lake Copais, in Boeotia in 1918.

have the development of a form which unites the bas-relief technique to that of sculpture in the round.

Another interesting comparison is that between two original marbles, both being female heads and of funerary figures. One is Attic, from the first half of the fourth century, and similar to those on the Elgin *stele,* although it is more delicately modelled and more finely expressive; the other is already Hellenistic (her sister, from Tarsus, is in the Louvre and it is likely that this is from the same city or, in any event, from a workshop on the coast of Asia-Minor). The features are larger, the relief more accentuated, the expression more open.

We will not linger over the Lansdowne *Heracles,* an excellent and well-known replica of the *Heracles* of Scopas. It can be ranked with the head of a young man with curly hair, of approximately the same date, which is closely related to the Ludovisi *Ares*– debatably either from Scopas or Lysippus. Another piece from Scopas seems to be the head of Venus (Capitoline type), a late replica not earlier than the Antonine period, but whose face was sculpted by a sensitive hand, as we can see from the modelling of the slightly smiling lips.

We come to the end of the Hellenistic period with the extraordinarily fresh feminine bust which is of the type of the Herculaneum Girl and can be dated from the hairstyle to the last years of the fourth century BC. This is not exactly a replica, for the tilt of the head is different; it is rather a personal and happy re-working of an original creation which enjoyed considerable success.

We get another glimpse of youthful grace in the statue of the torso of a very young girl. This seems like a vision of an actual model and is a perfect

(continued page 73)

◄ WOMAN'S HEAD

Parian Marble. Height: 11 ins. Width: 11 ins.

c. 300 B C

A female figure with curled hair surmounted by a crown of braids. Originally from Asia Minor.

◄ LION

Marble. Height: 44¼ ins. Width: 24 ins. Length: 67¼ ins.

3rd or 2nd Century B C

This lion with half-open mouth and damaged paws originates from Asia Minor. Probably a Hellenistic funerary piece.

VENUS ►

Marble. Height: 10¾ ins.

3rd Century B C

The upper part of a statue of a girl; a charming work of the early Hellenistic period. The body is delicately modelled and the hair-style is simple with two braids falling to the shoulders.

◄ CROUCHING VENUS

Marble. Height: 45 ins.

Roman replica.

This Venus is a Roman replica of a Greek original of the 3rd Century BC attributed to Doidalses. Similar replicas are in the Metropolitan Museum, the Museo delle Terme and the Louvre, though all in less good condition. On the replica in the Louvre (Salle des Cariatides, No. 2240), known as the Vénus de Vienne (Isère), the figure is headless and only the hand of Eros remains.

Collections: Sir Francis Cook, Doughty House, Richmond; Lord Anson; Cavaceppi. Purchased in 1955.

Bibliography: W. R. VALENTINER and P. WESCHER, *The J. Paul Getty Museum Guidebook*, p. 11. For the Vénus de Vienne, cf. E. COCHE DE LA FERTÉ, *La sculpture grecque et romaine au Musée du Louvre*, Paris, 1951, p. 36–38, fig. p. 39.

◄ APHRODITE

Bronze. Height: 5¾ ins.

Alexandria; 2nd Century B C

This figurine on its round base is remarkable for the elegance of its movement. Aphrodite is caught putting on her necklace. This attitude recalls familiar classical subjects of the antique period, the prototype being probably the Pselimene of Praxiteles described by Pliny. This model survived through the Hellenistic period to the Empire and is known in many examples, the most obvious being those in the British Museum (4th Century) and the Metropolitan Museum.

Bibliography: P. WESCHER, 'New Acquisitions 1956–57', *Bulletin of the J. Paul Getty Museum*, vol. 1, pp. 15–16, fig. 7a., cf. M. BIEBER, *The Sculptures of the Hellenistic Age*, which illustrates on plate 36 the British Museum figurine.

HEAD OF A BOY ▲

Marble. Height: 11 ins.

Roman; period of Hadrian

This lovely head with thick curls falling in a fringe across the forehead is very similar to the heads of Antinous, Hadrian's favourite.

◄ DIANA THE HUNTRESS WITH A DOG AND A STAG

Bronze. Height: Diana: 11¾ ins., Dog: 4¼ ins., Stag: 3¾ ins.

Probably Roman; 1st Century B C

This group is composed of three elements: Diana, a dog with raised head, and a stag which is considerably smaller than the dog. Diana wears a tunic and has a rolled animal's pelt like a girdle just below the line of her breasts. The two arms, added later, may not have belonged originally to this figure. A classic example of Artemis the Huntress, a model originally designed in the 4th Century by Greek sculptors. The most famous replica of this original is the Artemis known as the Diane de Versailles now in the Louvre.

Bibliography: P. WESCHER, 'New Acquisitions 1956–1957', *Bulletin of the J. Paul Getty Museum*, vol. I, p. 12–13. For the Diane de Versailles, cf. M. BIEBER, *The Sculptures of the Hellenistic Age*, p. 63, fig. 201, and E. COCHE DE LA FERTÉ, *La sculpture grecque et romaine au Museé du Louvre*, Paris, 1951, p. 40.

introduction to Hellenistic realism, the child's features and the detailed modelling of the torso are new to Greek art. There is a striking resemblance to the young Niobide supported by her brother in the Vatican Museum, which suggests a similar date at the beginning of the third century BC.

The most realistic and forceful example in classical art of a female nude was the *Crouching Aphrodite* of Doidalses of Bythnia. One of the best replicas of this comes from the Doughty House Collection. It is not of course certain that the fragmentary child attached to the goddess was present in the original. It is small in relation to the ample proportions of the principal figure and this suggests that it may well be an addition by a Roman copyist.

Cornelius Vermeule has revealed the importance of a recent acquisition of the Malibu Museum to the art of the second half of the third century BC: a helmeted head, which goes with the body of Achilles in the group made up of the Greek hero and his victim, the Amazon Penthesilia. The original of this Pergamon group, damaged copies of which are to be found in three museums in Rome, was doubtless a companion piece to the famous group of Menelaus and Patroclus. These two groups, whose inspiration was erudite and literary, were made to celebrate the permanence of the Hellenistic victory in Asia, in conformity with the ambitions of the kings of Pergamos.

We know that Roman sculpture was responsible for few original creations but that it excelled in portraiture. There are few strictly Roman sculptures in the Getty Museum, but the three portraits to be found there are among the best produced by Roman art. The seated statue, discovered in Rome during the sixteenth century, is a rare example of a Roman matron as the goddess Cybele. The cult of this oriental goddess was approved by Claudius and, since the hair styling indicates the Julian-Claudian era, this imposing statue must date from the reign of that Emperor. The monumental character of this portrait and the fact that the figure is disguised as a

(continued page 76)

◄ HERACLES

Pentelic marble. Height: 76¼ ins.

Roman replica; 1st Century B C–1st Century A D

A Roman replica of a work by Scopas, under the influence of Lysippus. Often taken for a Hellenistic work. Heracles is shown as a young man with the usual attributes: a club and a lion's skin.

Collections: Discovered at Hadrian's Villa, Tivoli, property of Count Fede, in 1790; Marefoschi; Jenkins; Lord Lansdowne (since 1792).

Bibliography: WAAGEN, *Art treasures in Great Britain*, p. 11, 1854; A. D. MICHAELIS, *Ancient Marbles in Great Britain*, pp. 451–452; CLARAC, *Musée de Sculpture*, vol. V; FURTWANGLER, *Masterpieces of Greek Sculptures*, 1894; RODENWALT, *Die Kunst der Antike*, 1927; G. M. A. RICHTER, *The Sculpture and the Sculptors of the Greeks*, New Haven, 1950, pp. 180–274, fig. 707; L. CURTIUS, *Die Antike Kunst*, vol. 11, 1938, p. 407; J. CHARBONNEAUX, *La sculpture grecque*.

◄ ROMAN WOMAN AS CYBELE

Marble. Height: 63¾ ins.

Roman; 1st Century AD

Roman women of the best society sometimes had their portraits done in the guise of their favourite goddesses, as here. Seated on a throne and wearing a turreted crown from which hangs a veil, and holding in her left hand a sheaf of wheat, this matron is surrounded by the attributes of Cybele and Ceres: on her left, a horn of plenty and on her right, a lion.

Collection: Mattei (16th Century), Rome: Gavin Hamilton (18th Century; Duke of Buckingham, Stowe, Buckinghamshire; Lord Lonsdale, Lowther Castle, from 1848 (the statue was for a long time known as the *Lowther Cybele*).

Bibliography: A. VENUTI, *Vetera Monumenta Matthaeiorum*, vol. 1, Rome, 1779, pl. 23; H. R. FORSTER, *Stowe Collection Catalogue*, London, 1948, p. 264, No. 21; CLARAC, *Musée de sculpture*, vol. III, Paris, 1850, 664 E, pl. 396 A; D. MICHAELIS, *Ancient Marbles in Great Britain*, Cambridge, 1882, p. 498, No. 21; Cornelius C. VERMEULE, 'A Statue of a Roman Lady as a Cybele', *Bulletin of the J. Paul Getty Museum*, vol. 1, 1957, pp. 22–25, fig. 10.

divinity justifies our concluding that it represents an Empress. Its resemblance to the black stone head of Agrippina in the Ny-Carlsberg Glyptothek in Copenhagen allows us to suggest that it is of this same redoubtable Empress, wife of Claudius and mother of Nero, an identification which has an important historical significance. The other two portraits are excellent examples of iconographic sculpture at the end of the Flavian era and the beginning of the reign of Hadrian. Apart from their quality, they are of interest because they are both nearly intact and precisely dated. The portrait of Julia shows her in a diadem and veiled. It is thus a posthumous portrait of the daughter of Titus, who died in 90 AD at the age of twenty. She was proclaimed august during her lifetime and divine after her death – hence the diadem and the veil. The features of the young woman seem to be somewhat idealized and strengthened. The more flowing and subtle modelling of the preceding period tends to become rigid and points toward the incisive severity of the style of the Trajan period.

We may observe the opposite process in the bust of Sabina, wife of the Emperor Hadrian. Sabina was approximately thirty two years of age when her husband came to the throne in 117 AD, at which time she received the title Augusta which gave her the right to wear the diadem. The slight wearing of the marble doubtless adds somewhat to the softness of the modelling. However, it is nonetheless true that here is an example of a very different style than that which was common under the reign of Trajan. From an historical view point – thanks to this portrait – it is possible to affirm that, from the beginning of his reign, Hadrian's philhellenism was clearly manifested and affirmed through a return to classical Greek art. One detail is of particular significance: the hairstyle. Before 117 AD, Sabina wore her hair in a fan of curls laboriously arranged above her forehead, a style little changed during Trajan's time and which went back to the Flavian epoch. It is altogether probable that the new Emperor had the Empress adopt the classical coiffure – waved and parted in the middle – of the Greek goddesses of the fifth and fourth centuries BC. Furthermore, there can be little doubt that Hadrian called in a Greek sculptor to create this portrait, which had the force of a manifesto. Aside from the purity of the style, particularly evident in the drawing of the eyes, one detail seems to me characteristic: the foliated double scroll, of an extreme fineness, which decorates the diadem, its curves starting from a stylized lotus-flower placed exactly above the centre parting in the hair. This is an Attic characteristic. This moving, warm and human portrait is yet another example of that taste for the classical Greek style which is the dominant note in the Getty Museum's collection of antique art.

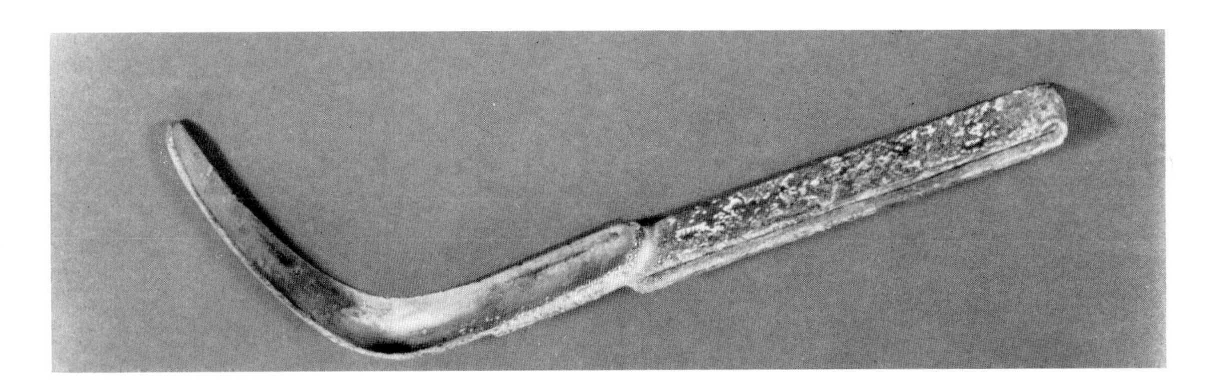

HEAD OF JULIA DAUGHTER OF TITUS ▸

Marble. Height: 13 ins. without base, 19¼ ins. with base.

1st Century A D

Julia, daughter of the Emperor Titus, is shown here with her intricately curled hair arranged in a fan-shape around her forehead. She herself probably introduced this style in Rome; it appears in the busts of several great Roman women of this period. Another bust of Julia Titi is in the National Museum of Rome. The identification of the bust in the Uffizi Florence, is doubtful.

Bibliography: For other busts, cf. Anton HECKLER; *Greek and Roman Portraits,* London, 1912, pl. p. 238.

◂ STRIGILE

Bronze. Length: 8½ ins.

Roman; c. 100 A D

This is a scraping tool used in ancient times for removing dust or sweat from the skin after exercising or bathing. The present example has a hand grip (clausula) and a curved blade, decorated probably by the artisan.

◄ VENUS PUNISHING CUPID

Roman bronze. Height: 11½ ins.

Antonine period 2nd Century A D

Venus, naked and wearing a diadem, holds in her upraised right hand an object said to be a fan (catalogue of the Lehman Collection), a sandal or – more likely – a roll of fabric (Paul Wescher). With her left hand she threatens a tiny winged Eros, also standing. Most unusually, the group is on its original base.

Collection: Lehmann (sold by the Hôtel Drouat, 11 June 1925, No. 120).

Bibliography: Catalogue des Antiquités, Collection Lehman, Paris, 1925, pl. XIV, No. 120, p. 27; Salomon REINACH, *Répertoire de la statuaire grecque et romaine,* Paris, 1930, vol. VI, p. 83, 2; Karl-Anton NEUGEBAUER, 'Die Venus von Grenoble', *Pantheon,* vol. XVII, Jan.–June 1936, p. 50, fig. 4; P. WESCHER, 'New Acquisitions', *Bulletin of the J. Paul Getty Museum,* vol. 1, p. 15.

WOMAN'S HEAD ►

Parian marble. Height: 14¼ ins.

Alexandria

This head, with empty eye-sockets, is remarkable for its beauty and facial expression. According to Jean Charbonneaux, it is Roman of the time of Hadrian or the Antonines (2nd Century A D). A fine replica of the Capitoline Aphrodite.

◄ FLUTE PLAYER

Bas-relief. Height: 19 3/4 ins. Width: 12 1/2 ins.

Roman

The flutist is shown standing, his right leg slightly drawn back; he is naked save for a cloak tied round the neck and thrown back over the shoulders. He is playing a double flute. This bas-relief, larger at its base than at the top, may have served to hold a candelabra.

ACHILLES ►

Marble. Height: 16 1/2 ins.

End of 2nd Century or beginning of 3rd Century A D

C. C. Vermeule has shown that this must be a head of Achilles wearing a helmet and was part of a group showing the famous warrior supporting the Amazon Queen Penthesilea. It seems to be a Roman replica of a Hellenistic prototype executed at Pergamo in 117 BC. According to this hypothesis, the torso belonging to this replica is in the Musée des Beaux Arts in Geneva and other fragments in the Museo delle Terme in Rome.

Purchased in London. Probably from a large British collection of the late 18th Century.

Bibliography: C. C. VERMEULE: 'Achilles and Penthesilea. A new discovery in Hellenistic Sculpture'. *Bulletin of the J. Paul Getty Museum*, No. 2.

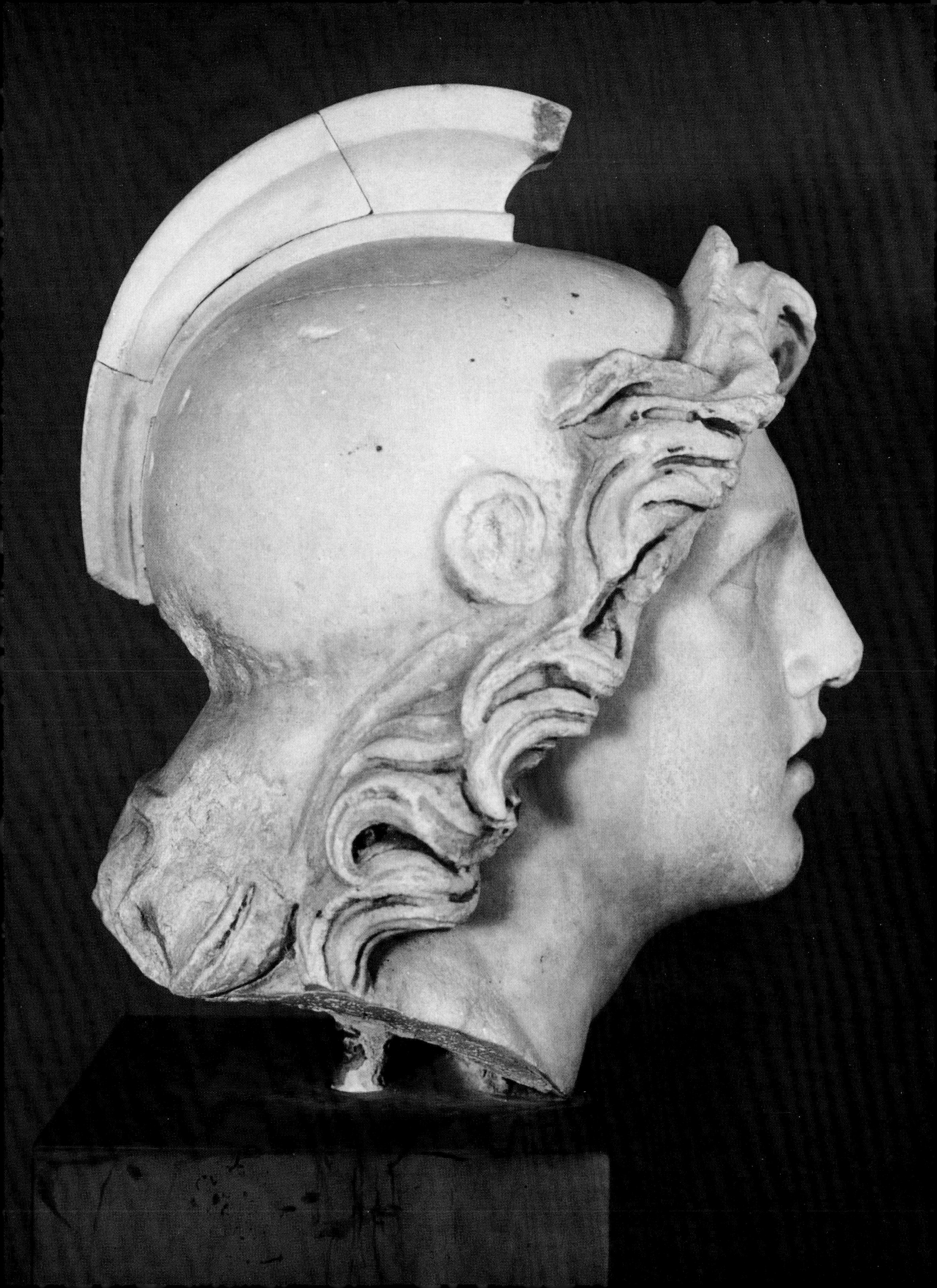

◀ GODDESS (?)

Limestone. Height: 22 ins.

Said to come from Carthage, but unlike any other Carthaginian works. Gilbert Charles-Picard suggests that it may be a Coptic piece imported from Egypt. Rather coarsely carved, the block having been hollowed out and worked with an auger; the eyes were drilled. Covered with a cape which forms a sort of niche around her. Probably the figure of a goddess.

THE LEGEND OF ORPHEUS ▶

Gallo-Roman mosaic. 191 3/4 ins. x 139 ins.

2nd or 3rd Century AD

The central motif shows a circle within a square. Feminine figures at the four corners. Within the circle formed by a twisted cord in red and black are six hexagonal medallions (animals) grouped around a central hexagon (Orpheus).

Purchased by A Barsanti. W. R. Hearst Collection (sale, Hammer Gallery, New York, 1941).

Bibliography: Sales Catalogue of the Hammer Galleries, N. Y., p. 329. W. R. VALENTINER and P. WESCHER, *The J. Paul Getty Museum Guidebook*, p. 16. According to a letter from Mr. Franklin M. Biebel, Director of the Frick Collection, New York, this mosaic can be dated to the 2nd or 3rd Century AD. The same geometric disposition of various elements can be found in a mosaic of Sainte-Colombe (cf. G. LAFAYE, *Inventaire des mosaïques de la Gaule barbonnaise*, 1909, No. 217) and in a mosaic discovered at the Porta Pia in Rome, now in the Vatican Museum (cf. Marian E. BLAKE, 'Roman Mosaïcs of the Second Century', *Memoirs of the American Academy in Rome*, vol. 13, 1939, pl. 26–2). The four figures in the corners represent the four seasons.

BUST OF SABINA ▸

Marble. Height: 17 ins.

Rome; 2nd Century A D

Originally identified as a bust of Livia by Dr Speyer of the Vatican Museum and Professor Rizzo. Hence datable to the end of the First Century B C. Jean Charbonneaux has identified it as Sabina, wife of the Emperor Hadrian; it is the most beautiful of the few known busts of her (cf. the bust in the Museo delle Terme). The work thus dates from the 2nd Century A D and is in the neo-classical style of that period, further evidence of which is to be found in the delicate scroll-work of the diadem, which is typical of the pseudo-Attic style of the Hadrianic era.

PAINTINGS

by

JULIUS S. HELD

[Professor of Art History]

[Barnard College, Columbia University, New York City]

SCHOOL OF PAOLO UCCELLO

▲ BATTLE SCENE

Florence, middle of the 15th Century

Panel. Height: 17¼ ins. Width: 65 ins.

This front panel of a cassone or marriage chest is attributed to the Master of the Battle of Anghiari, a painter of the school of Uccello (1396–1475). It depicts the Siege of Troy: Achilles, after having withdrawn into his tent (extreme left) and refusing to do battle, learns of the death of Patroclus and returns to the fight to avenge his friend (left of the ramparts). According to the method of continued narration which was to die out in the course of the Renaissance, the different episodes of the battle follow from left to right. The transition between the different periods of the combat is made by means of recurring scenes (Achilles in his tent, two lancers on the ramparts). Here, however, along with this medieval conception, we see a preoccupation with perspective which is evident from the architecture of the ramparts.

Collections: Bardini, Florence; M. Bellini, Florence. Acquired June, 1953.

Exhibitions: Laurent le Magnifique, Palazzo Strozzi, Florence, 1951.

Bibliography: W. R. VALENTINER and P. WESCHER, *The J. Paul Getty Museum Guidebook*, Los Angeles, 1954, p. 24; A. C., 'Una fronte di Cassone di Paolo Uccello', *Arte figurativa antica e moderna*, Milan, Jan.-Feb. 1954, No. 7, p. 28, fig. 1, 3, and 4; Ethel LE VANE and J. Paul Getty *Collector's Choice*, London, 1955, pp. 207, 227–9; W. R. VALENTINER and P. WESCHER, op. cit., pp. 17–18.

Prior to the world-wide publicity that accompanied his acquisition of Rubens' *Diana,* Mr Getty's collection of paintings was little known. This is not surprising. Although it does contain many fine pieces and a few of truly superior merit, most of the paintings are remarkable for their intimate charm rather than for spectacular appearance or historical prominence. Mr Getty himself is aware of the limitations of his interest in paintings. His passionate desire to own a certain work of art has been more often aroused by classical sculpture and eighteenth-century furniture and tapestries. Still, a certain degree of excitement must have accompanied the purchase of Rembrandt's *Marten Looten* and Gainsborough's portrait of *James Christie,* and no work of art has occupied his thought more relentlessly than Raphael's *Madonna of Loreto*

Yet this is no longer the issue. In view of the fact that a large part of the collection is being made accessible through this publication, and through exhibition in a museum, it is less important to speculate what acquisition and ownership may have meant to Mr Getty himself than to know how these works affect the lovers of art all over the world. Whatever their impact, they will make it as a group; no matter where they came from and when they were bought, they are now linked to each other by virtue of the fate of being part of one collection.

It would be less than ingenuous to say that this collection forms a harmonious

(continued page 90)

BENVENUTO DI GIOVANNI (1436 – c. 1518)

◄ NATIVITY

Panel. Height: 22¼ ins. Width: 15½ ins.

Sienese School, 15th Century

Collections: Sir Philip Burne-Jones; Samuel Untermeyer, Yonkers. Acquired 10 May 1940, at the Parke-Bernet Gallery Untermeyer Sale, No. 48.

The painting was originally attributed to Girolamo di Benvenuto but has been re-attributed to Benvenuto di Giovanni by Professor Federico Zeri.

Bibliography: LE VANE and GETTY, op. cit., pp. 212, 226; VALENTINER and WESCHER, op. cit., 1956, p. 19; R. van MARLE, The Development of the Italian Schools of Painting, XVI, The Hague, 1937, p. 407, fig. 235, (there given to Benvenuto di Giovanni) A similar painting at Montepulciano (Tuscany) is reproduced in the same volume, p. 432, fig. 250.

GIROLAMO DI BENVENUTO (1470–1524)

NATIVITY ►

Panel. Height: 77½ ins. Width: 63⅛ ins.

Sienese School, 15th Century

Collection: Van Gelder, Brussels. Acquired August, 1954.

The painting was originally attributed to Benvenuto di Giovanni but has been re-attributed to Girolamo di Benvenuto by Professor Federico Zeri.

Bibliography: LE VANE and GETTY, op. cit., p. 226; VALENTINER and WESCHER, op. cit., 1956, pp. 18–19.

whole. There is a certain unevenness both in the distribution of schools and in the level of artistic performance. Like the members of a party, the pictures gather into groups, some large, some small; there are also a few poor mixers who stand apart. The few Quattrocento pieces form a little clique by themselves, restrained and withdrawn in their cool, virginal colour and emotional innocence. The Flemish pictures betray their kinship with the Italian works of the Renaissance; Rubens' inspired sensuousness has more in common, surely, with Titian and Tintoretto, and even with Lotto and Cariani, than with the more prosaic art of the contemporary Dutch. The Dutch actually are by far the most numerous. Here is real companionableness, a common spirit of earthy realism, affectionately extolling the beauty of nature and the wholesomeness of man's appetites. The portrait of Louis XIV by Rigaud, by contrast, stands alone and at the museum of the Ranch House has wisely been placed in the vicinity of the French eighteenth-century room with its tapestries and inlaid furniture. Anywhere else it might have overwhelmed its less ostentatious neighbours.

The beginning, chronologically, is marked by two Florentine *cassoni,* originally made for the decoration of chests. One, from the school of Francesco di Giorgio, represents the Triumph of Chastity based on Petrarch's *Trionfi.* It is a gay little panel, flanked by two swan-like griffins in relief, holding armorial shields still unidentified. The other by the so-called Master of the Anghiari Battle reflects the style of Uccello in the crisp, geometrically stylised silhouettes of the figures and the poster-like simplicity of its colour-areas. Despite the somewhat mechanical motions of horses and men, and the down-scaled size of the houses and hills, the panel conveys well the confused bustle of a battle-scene that–somewhat unexpectedly–commemorates the Siege of Troy.

In contrast to the busy air of the *cassoni,* Girolamo di Benvenuto's altarpiece is a study in hieratic grandeur and symmetry. Even the rocks of the cave where–according to the accounts of apocryphal gospels–Christ was born, seem to have been arranged in worshipping groups, as if under a spell. The Virgin, undoubtedly, is the dominant figure. She admirably combines humility with quiet dignity. Joseph, by contrast, though strong and handsome in a rustic way, is a marginal figure, not participating in the action which connects the Virgin with the solemn Christ Child on the ground.

(continued page 94)

LORENZO DI CREDI (1459–1537)

MADONNA, CHILD, AND ANGEL ▶

Florence, painted c. 1480

Panel. Height: 27 3/8 ins. Width: 18 3/4 ins.

This painting of Lorenzo di Credi or his school is reminiscent of the altar front at Pistoia begun by Verrochio and finished by his pupil Lorenzo di Credi. Degenhart attributes it to Giovanni di Benedetto Cianfanini (born in 1462), a pupil of Lorenzo di Credi. He points out that the landscape at the upper right (a mill with a river on which two swans are swimming) is a copy of a landscape in the background of a painting by Memling (no. 3244 in the Uffizi).

Collections: Old Pinakothek, Munich, which acquired it in Florence, 1891. Acquired December, 1953.

Bibliography: Katalog der Älteren Pinakothek, Munich, 1908, p. 214; CROWE and CAVALCASELLE, *A History of Painting In Italy,* ed. Borenius, 1914, VI, p. 42; Bernhard DEGENHART, 'Die Schüler des Lorenzo di Credi', *Münchner Jahrbuch,* New series, Munich, 1932, p. 140; *Katalog der Älteren Pinakothek,* Munich, 1936, p. 57; VALENTINER and WESCHER, op. cit., 1956, p. 18.

TITIAN (1477–1576)

PENITENT ST MAGDALEN ▲

Painted c. 1561–1565

Canvas. Height: 41 3/4 ins. Width: 36 ins.

The Pitti Gallery in Florence contains a St Magdalen by Titian dated 1530 which is identical save for the abundance of coiffure. The painting in the Hermitage in Leningrad (painted circa 1565) would seem contemporary with the present example; the clothing is identical. But the background landscape on the right is different in each example and does not appear in the version of 1530. In the present example it has greater depth than the painting in Leningrad.

Collection: Otto Gutekunst, London. Acquired in 1956.

Exhibitions: Venetian Art in Stockholm, (Konstens Venedig), 20 Oct. 1962–10 Feb. 1963, No. 98.

Bibliography: VALENTINER and WESCHER, op. cit., 1956, p. 20; Bernard BERENSON, *Italian Pictures of the Renaissance, Venetian School,* London, 1957, I, p. 190; Benedict NICOLSON, 'Venetian Art in Stockholm', *Burlington Magazine,* CV, Jan. 1963, p. 32. For comparisons with the other paintings see: Oskar FISCHEL, 'Tizian', *Klassiker der Kunst,* Stuttgart–Berlin, 1904, pl. 57 (Florence), pl. 187 (Hermitage).

GIOVANNI CARIANI
(1485–90 – about 1547)

PORTRAIT OF AN UNKNOWN GENTLEMAN ▶

Canvas. Height: 29 1/8 ins. Width: 24 3/4 ins.

Venice, 16th Century

Sometimes attributed to Giorgione, who influenced Giovanni Busi, known as Cariani, this portrait shows a three-quarter view of an unidentified man, around 35 to 40 years of age, wearing a fur cap and touching a sword with his gloved right hand.

Collections: Robert H. Benson, London; Lord Duveen; Count Foresto, Milan. Acquired May, 1953.

Exhibitions: New Gallery, London, 1894–5, No. 230; Royal Academy Winter Exhibition, London, 1896, No. 163; 'The Venetian School', The Burlington Fine Arts Club, London, 1914, No. 28.

Bibliography: W. von SEIDLITZ, 'Die Ausstellung venezianischer Kunst in der New Gallery zu London im Winter 1894–5', *Repertorium für Kunstwissenschaft,* XVIII 1895, p. 214; G. GRONAU, 'L'art vénitien à Londres', *Gazette des Beaux Arts,* ser. III, XIII, Paris, 1895, p. 438; B. BERENSON, *The Study and Criticism of Italian Art,* London, 1901, I, p. 140, n. 1; Lionel CUST, 'La Collection de M. R. H. Benson', *Les Arts,* LXX, Oct. 1907, p. 16; CROWE and CAVALCASELLE, *The History of Painting in North Italy,* ed. Borenius, New. York, 1912, III, p. 460; *The Venetian School, Pictures By Titian and His Contemporaries,* Burlington Fine Arts Club, London, 1915, pp. 47–8; A. VENTURI, *Storia dell'Arte Italiana,* Milan, 1928, IX, part III, p. 454, fig. 297; G. TROCHE, 'Giovanni Cariani als Bildnismaler', *Pantheon,* IX, 1932, p. 7; G. TROCHE, 'Giovanni Cariani', *Jahrbuch der Preußischen Kunstsammlungen,* Berlin, LV, 1934, p. 122; VALENTINER and WESCHER, op. cit., 1954, p. 26; LE VANE and GETTY, op. cit., pp. 207–9; B. BERENSON, *Italian Pictures of the Renaissance, Venetian School,* London, 1957, I, p. 55.

The broken column behind the Virgin may be the one on which – according to the Pseudo-Bonaventure – the Virgin supported herself in the hour of Christ's birth. Since Christ's passion is alluded to in the central circle of the predella, it may also refer to Christ's Flagellation, in keeping with the widely read Revelations of St Bridget of Sweden. That it is broken, is a symbolical feature referring to the pre-Christian world from the ruins of which will arise a new order under grace.

Less austere than his son's work is a Nativity by Benvenuto di Giovanni, done in the tender, though somewhat conservative manner of the 15th century Sienese School. The last Quattrocento picture featuring a rather girlish Madonna, may be a Giovanni di Benedetto Cianfanini though traditionally attributed to his teacher Lorenzo di Credi. It is remarkable for its exceptionally fine state of preservation and the unusual iconographic detail of a glass filled with an arrangement of spring flowers.

Foremost among the paintings of the High Renaissance is a version of Raphael's so-called *Madonna of Loreto* which most experts consider to be by the master's own hand. The painting, unfortunately, has not come down in perfect condition. Much of the original surface has been lost through later over-cleaning. The impression of the picture, nevertheless, has regained a good deal of its original strength since the removal through skilful cleaning of some clumsy repaintings. The claims of the panel to be the original are negatively supported by the blatant inferiority of all other existing versions; they are reinforced, besides some more technical observations, by the quality of the preliminary chalk lines seen in infra-red photos, and the presence of *pentimenti,* most noticeable in the Virgin's right hand. As it is, the picture still justifies Vasari's high praise: "He (the Christ Child) is so beautiful in body and facial expression that everything in him proclaims the true Son of God and no less beautiful are the face and the head of the Virgin; and beyond that supreme beauty one can also see her joy and piety". There is also a Saint Joseph, leaning with both hands on a stick, who is thoughtfully watching the King and Queen of Heaven with the admiration of a truly saintly old man.)

The same period is also represented by a distinguished group of portraits. The earliest is Lotto's monumental *Portrait of Gian Pietro Crivelli,* a jeweller who is holding a box with rings in his left hand, while showing – or offering – a single one with his right. It is obvious that he is a man of substance, in every sense of the word, and that the rings are included for his identification rather than as an advertisement. He

(continued page 98)

RAFFAELO SANZIO (1483–1520)

MADONNA OF LORETO ▶

Painted 1508–09

Panel. Height: 37 ins. Width: 35 7/8 ins.

The text of the legend will be found on page 66.

Collections: Bourbon, Tuileries 1830, Bourbon, Frohsdorf (1830–1938). Sold at Sotheby's 20 July 1938 by Princess Beatrice Bourbon Massimo.

Exhibitions: National Gallery, London, 1965. Exhibited as the Madonna of Loreto.

Bibliography: Vasari 'De Vite'; Von Sandrart 'Die Deutsche Academie' Nuremberg 1675; Vögelin 'Die Madonna von Loreto' 1870; Crowe & Cavalcaselle 'Raphael' t. II 1885; J. Pfau, Die Madonna von Loreto, Zürich, 1922; A. Scharf 'Raphael and the Getty Madonna' Apollo, February 1964. Cecil Gould, Trophy of Conquest – the Musée Napoleon and the Creation of the Louvre – London 1965, pp. 47, 124.

If some parts of the picture in the Getty collection have been damaged and restored – such as the face of Saint Joseph –; A. Scharf thinks that the head and hands of the Virgin are intact and that the delicacy of their design indicates an original work, a theory confirmed by an X-ray examination of the Panel, which reveals many 'Pentimenti', corrections which a copyist would have neither the patience to reproduce, nor would the idea occur to him.
Mr. Federico Zeri says 'The Madonna's face points towards Raphael's middle period around 1507–08, while in all the other versions the types are translated into Raphael's very late grammar. Moreover, the Getty panel shows in the Madonna a strong influence of Leonardo, a fact which is entirely missing from the remaining examples of the same composition.'
Princess Nieves Bourbon Massimo, for her part, states in a letter addressed to J. P. Getty on May 19th 1964, that she remembers having seen this picture in the bedroom of her uncle, Jaime III of Bourbon, in the Castle of Frohsdorf, where she lived for several years.
As we know, this castle became the home of the exiled Bourbons after the revolution of 1830 and nearly all the pictures, there, come from the Tuileries. The Madonna di Loreto, most probably, hung in the King's Bedroom at the Tuileries.

Commissioned by Pope Julius II for the church of Santa Maria del Popolo in Rome. This is undoubtedly the composition by Raphael described by Vasari. For a long time it was thought that the original was lost.
In the issue of Apollo of February 1964, Dr. Alfred Scharf devoted a long and minute study to this picture. Having first recalled that a note in Il Codice Magliabechiano (about 1544) mentions a Holy Family by Raphael, which was, at the time, in the church of Santa Maria del Popolo in Rome, a picture described by Vasari on several occasions, and also having mentioned an inscription according to which an identical composition formed part of the treasure of the Casa Santa di Loreto in 1717, Alfred Scharf establishes that the picture in the Getty collection is truly the original of a work which enjoyed a considerable success, as is seen by the thirty odd copies, of which the best known are in the Louvre (attributed to Giulio Romano) and in the Chantilly Museum (attributed to Penni).

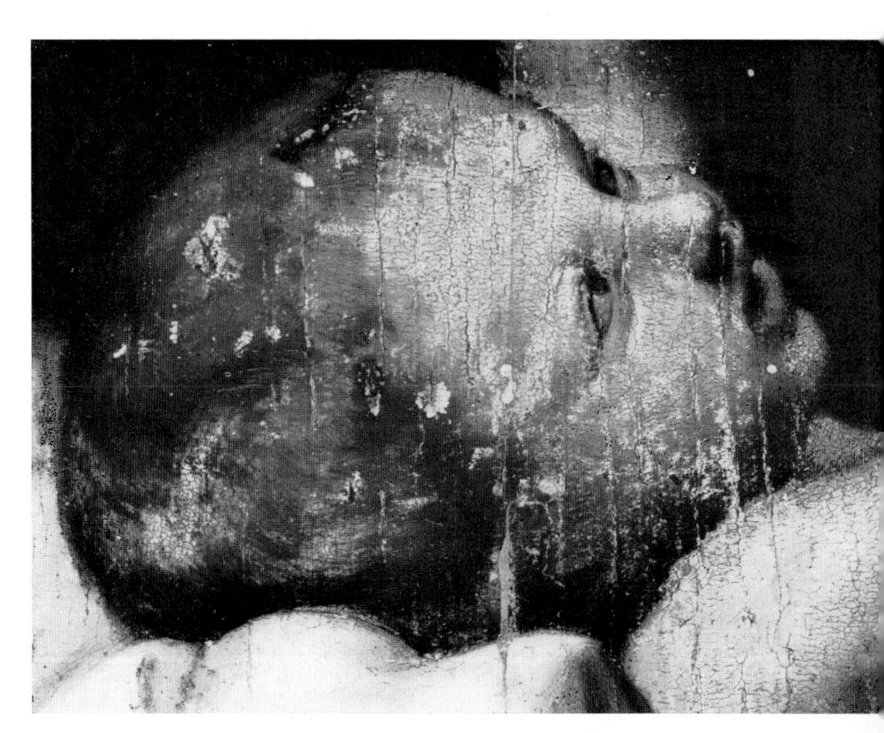

may be proud of his craftsmanship, but the artist stresses above all the air of self confidence of a gentleman who is sure of his status. It is not accidental that his glance seems to go above our heads into the distance, thus projecting gently but unmistakably a sense of social superiority and exclusiveness.

Cariani's *Portrait of an Unknown Gentleman* is very different in feeling. There is a dreamy, almost moody expression on the young man's face. Despite the prominence given to his sword, this it not a martial figure. Whoever he was, in Cariani's portrayal he appears more like a poet or musician, a tender person not entirely unaware, it would seem, of the attraction he may have had for ladies. The artist had painted him first with a beret but changed it into a broadbrimmed hat presumably to balance the voluminous expanse of the mantle below.

A sheer delight, despite its less than perfect state of preservation, is the *Portrait of a Young Lady* attributed to Bonifazio Veronese, and again more recently also to Moretto da Brescia. The artist displays in full front view the majestic proportions then fashionable for young ladies and stressed by the costume rather than hidden. A wide, generous décolleté covers a bosom of ample shape below the grand sweep of the shoulders. In the middle of this large area the rising lines of a thin golden necklace gracefully lead the eye to the reserved and yet sensuously expectant face. While the centre of the composition is dominated by a few large areas of colour, the sides are enlivened by the intricate 'lattice-work' of the sleeves and the details of a romantic landscape featuring, probably for some definite reason, sections of ruined buildings.

A counterpart of this typically Venetian portrait is *The Lady Playing a Lute* by Bartolomeo Veneto, a picture which exists in several rather similar versions, all of

(continued page 104)

LORENZO LOTTO (About 1480 – about 1556)

PORTRAIT OF A JEWELLER ▶

Venetian School, c. 1519

Canvas. Height: 30 3/4 ins. Width: 25 1/8 ins.

Emma Zocca has recently identified this portrait as that of Gian Pietro Crivelli, a Milanese jeweller who posed for the artist in Rome during the latter's second visit there, when he was called to work at the Vatican in 1519. This identification is based on a document in the Vatican Archives.

Collections: Richard von Kaufmann, Berlin, purchased 1901, sold 1917; Robert Koch, Frankfort on the Main, 1925; Goudstikker, Amsterdam, 1934; R. von Hirsch, Basle, about 1953 (See Coletti); heirs of Louis Koch, Switzerland. Acquired from the Lotto exhibition at Venice, December 1953.

Exhibitions: 'Ausstellung von Meisterwerken alter Malerei aus Privatbesitz', Frankfurt, 1925, No. 123; 'Italiaansche Kunst In Nederlandsch Bezit', Stedelijk Museum, Amsterdam, 1934, No. 198; 'Mostra di Lorenzo Lotto', Palazzo Ducale, Venice, 1953, No. 33.

Bibliography: Gemälde des XIV–XVI Jahrhunderts aus der Sammlung Richard von Kaufmann, Berlin, 1901, p. 12; Emil WALDMAN, 'Leih-Ausstellung von Gemälden Alter Meister aus Frankfurter Privatbesitz', *Kunst und Künstler,* Sept. 1925, p. 483; Morton H. BERNATH, 'An Exhibition of Old Masters in Frankfurt', *Burlington Magazine,* XLVII, Oct. 1925, p. 216; A VENTURI, *Storia dell'Arte Italiana,* 1929, IX, part 4, p. 114; 'Italiaansche Kunst In Nederlandsch Bezit', Stedelijk Museum, Amsterdam, July 1–Oct. 1, 1934, p. 80; R. van MARLE, 'La Pittura all'Esposizione dell'Arte Antica Italiana di Amsterdam', *Bolletino d'Arte,* XXVIII, 1934–5, p. 396; A. BANTI and A. BOSCHETTO, *Lorenzo Lotto,* Florence, n. d., pp. 16, 24, 71; Luigi COLETTI, *Lotto,* Bergamo, 1953, p. 40; Emma ZOCCA, *Rivista dell'Istituto Nazionale D'Archeologia e Storia dell'Arte,* Rome, II, 1953, pp. 337–40; P. ZAMPETTI, ed., 'Mostra di Lorenzo Lotto', Palazzo Ducale, Venice, 1953, p. 58; B. BERENSON, *Lorenzo Lotto,* 1956, p. 36; VALENTINER and WESCHER, 1956, p. 19; B. BERENSON, *Italian Pictures of the Renaissance, Venetian School,* 1957, I, p. 105; C. GILBERT, *Art Journal,* XXI, 1962, p. 289.

BARTOLOMEO VENETO
(About 1480–1555)

◄ LADY PLAYING A LUTE

Panel. Height: 22 ins. Width: 16¼ ins.

Wrongly attributed to Leonardo in an inventory of the Charterhouse of Pavia, this gracious painting has been recognized as the portrait of Cecilia Galleriani of Milan, the mistress of Lodovico il Moro and the wife of the Count of Bergamo. She was celebrated for her beauty and for her musical ability. Two identical paintings are to be found in the Brera Pinakotek and the Gardner Museum, Boston.

Collections: Deposited at the Carthusian Monastery at Pavia after the imprisonment of Lodovico Il Moro until 1782; Count Giovanni Friziani, Milan. Acquired July, 1953.

Bibliography: LE VANE and GETTY, op. cit., pp. 227 and 231; VALENTINER and WESCHER, op. cit., 1956, p. 19; B. BERENSON, *Italian Pictures of The Renaissance, Venetian School*, I, p. 12. For the others mentioned see Angela OTTINO DELLA CHIESA, *Brera*, Novara, 1953, p. 48; Ph. HENDY, *The Isabella Stewart Gardner Museum*, Boston, 1931, pp. 28–30 (contains a list of ten versions).

BONIFAZIO VERONESE (1487–1553)

PORTRAIT OF A WOMAN ►

Canvas. Height: 42¼ ins. Width: 34½ ins.

Venetian School

Bonifazio Veronese, whose work is sometimes confused with that of his teachers Giorgione and Titian, has painted a young Venetian woman – whose identity remains a mystery – against a background of antique ruins.

Acquired from Luigi Bellini, Florence, November, 1953, as a Moretto de Brescia.

Exhibitions: Manchester City Art Gallery, Between Renaissance and Baroque – European Art – 1520–1600, 10th March to 6th April, 1965.

Bibliography: B. BERENSON, *Italian Pictures of the Renaissance, Venetian School*, London, 1957, I, p. 44 (listed with a question mark). *Manchester City Art Gallery Catalogue, Between Renaissance and Baroque, European Art 1520–1600, 1965*, pp. 18, 19, reproduced plate III. A note in the catalogue adds the following: – "The picture is obviously by the same hand as the 'Portrait of a Lady' in the Vienna Gallery (Inv. No. 1914) for which various attributions have been suggested. They are listed in detail in the Vienna Catalogue I, 1960, p. 72, No. 579, and include Bonifazio Veronese (Wickhoff), Sebastiano Florigerio (Gamba), G. B. Moroni (Ozzola), G. Savoldo (Boselli), F. Becaruzzi (Berenson), Moretto (Wilde, Fiocco, Baldass, Glück), collaboration of Lotto with Moretto or Moroni (Suida), Lotto (Morassi, Benesch). The latter attribution is also adopted by the Vienna catalogue of 1960. In the compiler's view only Bonifazio or Moretto can seriously be considered as authors of the Vienna and the Getty portraits."

TINTORETTO (1518–1594)

PORTRAIT OF DOGE PRIULI ▲

1560

Canvas. Height: 34 1/4 ins. Width: 26 1/4 ins.

Girolamo Priuli was Doge of Venice from 1559 to 1567. According to archives of the period (Lorenzi, Documenti 307), his portrait was made at the end of 1560. At the time, all official portraits were made in at least two versions. According to Berenson, there are three examples of this portrait: at the Academia in Venice, at the Detroit Institute of Art and in the J. Paul Getty Collection. Tintoretto also painted this subject in *The Doge Girolamo Priuli Receiving the Sword of Justice,* (Ducal Palace, Venice).

Collections: N. Rethmann. Acquired August 1954.

Bibliography: VALENTINER and WESCHER, op. cit., 1956, p. 20; B. BERENSON, *Italian Pictures of The Renaissance, Venetian School,* London, 1957, I, p. 178; For the Venice example, H. TIETZE, *Tintoretto,* London, 1948, p. 363.

TINTORETTO (1518–1594)

◀ ALLEGORY OF VANITY

Canvas. Height: 56 ins. Width: 42 1/8 ins.

This *Allegory of Vanity* probably formed part of a group in a Venetian palace and can be compared with the Allegory of Generosity formerly in the collection of Baron Louis de Rothschild (cf. B. Berenson, Venetian School, vol II, p. 1292). We find the same placing of a feminine figure seated near a tree and stretching out her arm which is covered with bracelets; in the present example, she is reaching for a mirror.

Collections: Sold at Christie's, London, 10 July 1953, No. 114. Acquired from Luigi Bellini, Florence, 1954.

Bibliography: Catalogue, 'Guinness and other Collections Sale', Christie's, London, July 10, 1953, p. 34; *Art Prices Current,* XXX, 1952–1953, p. A. 157, No 3865; VALENTINER and WESCHER, op. cit., 1956, pp. 20–21; B. BERENSON, *Italian Pictures of the Renaissance, Venetian School,* London, 1957, I, p. 178.

TINTORETTO (1518–1594)

TOILET OF VENUS ▶

Canvas. Height: 44 1/8 ins. Width: 39 3/8 ins.

Painted c. 1575–80

Titian undoubtedly created this type of Venus, seen from the back and to below the knees. Tintoretto was inspired by one of the many versions of Titian (such as the one in the National Gallery of Washington), but gives more life and movement to his subject. He undoubtedly made use of a living model posed in everyday surroundings, as shown by the window with lenticular panes at the left.

Collections: Duke of Sutherland; William Graham; Lady Horner; R. V. Kühlmann, Berlin. Acquired August, 1954.

Exhibitions: British Institution, London, 1838, No. 13.

Bibliography: D. von HADELN, 'Veronese's Venus At Her Toilet', *Burlington Magazine,* LIV, March, 1929, p. 116; Stephan POGLAYEN-NEUWALL, 'Titian's Pictures of The Toilet of Venus and Their Copies', *Art Bulletin,* XVI, Dec. 1934, p. 378; E. von der BERCKEN, *Jacopo Tintoretto,* Munich, 1942, No. 237, fig. 148; B. BERENSON, *Italian Pictures of the Renaissance, Venetian School,* London, 1957, I, p. 178; VALENTINER and WESCHER, op. cit., 1956, p. 20.

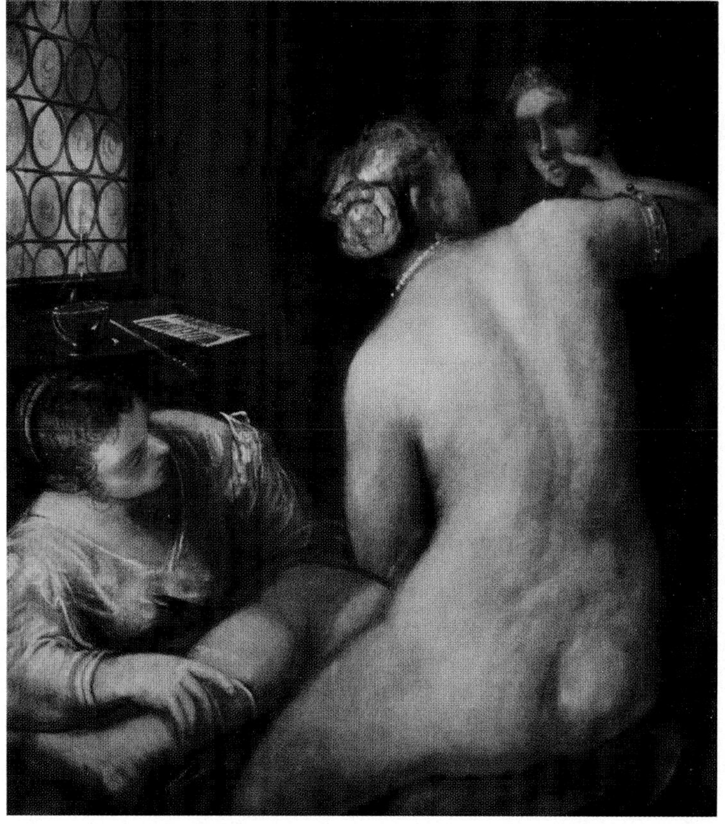

them reflecting a Milanese prototype influenced, if not actually formulated, by Leonardo da Vinci. The vaguely sentimental expression of the young lady is indicative of this influence, just as the careful execution of detail reflects the artist's acquaintance with transalpine art, especially Albrecht Dürer's.

Beautiful as these portraits are, they must yield in importance to the latest addition made to the Getty collection of paintings; Veronese's full-length portrait of a man which may actually be a self-portrait of the artist. Less than medium height and dressed severely in black, the model is given imposing dignity by the grandly proportioned piece of architecture against which he leans. The strong, if cool light crosses the right outline of the figure to echo from the stone in the form of a clearly silhouetted cast shadow; the same light illuminates the right corner of the building in an effective contrast to the colour of the costume. Three details of the setting pose intriguing problems of interpretation: between the visible sections of the two columns we perceive the bottom third of a – presumably allegorical – draped female figure; a Roman soldier forming part of a larger relief appears on the base below the right column; and in the wooded

ORAZIO LOMI, OR GENTILESCHI (1563–1639)

THE REST ON THE FLIGHT TO EGYPT ▸

Canvas. Height: 44¾ ins. Width: 64 ins.

The Virgin, seated on the ground, nurses the child Jesus, while St Joseph reclines in the background. This theme of the Holy Family inspired many paintings of Gentileschi; the example in the Louvre is very similar to this one but has an opening showing the sky in the left half of the painting. The example in the Louvre belonged to Louis XIV and was painted for Charles I of England. We know that Gentileschi spent the latter half of his life in London and died there. Benezit mentions a Holy Family painted for the Duke of Buckingham.

Collections: Formerly at Avington, and was one of those paintings given by George Villiers, Duke of Buckingham, to the Countess of Shrewsbury (Stowe Sale Catalogue); with Richard Grenville, second Duke of Buckingham and Chandos, K. G., 1848, the collection was sold at the Stowe Sale, 13 Sept. 1848, No. 152; Montague Parker, of Whiteway, Devonshire, 1848; Sir Harold Farquhar, London. Acquired 1953.

Exhibitions: 'Autumn Exhibition of Fine Pictures By Old Masters', Agnew's, London, Oct.–Dec., 1951, No. 26.

Bibliography: VALENTINER and WESCHER, op. cit., 1954, p. 25. For the Louvre painting: HAUTECŒUR, ed., *Catalogue of Paintings in the Louvre,* Paris, II, 1926, p. 74.

landscape at the far back the artist sketched somewhat out of context but unmistakably the graceful outlines of Venice's own Cathedral of St. Mark's.

Besides the portraits, to which should still be added Veronese's delightful study of a youth and Tintoretto's patriarchal rendering of Doge Girolamo Priuli, there are also sixteenth-century canvases of religious and allegorical subjects. Most important is Titian's *Magdalen*—a composition that must have been very popular as it exists in several versions. The Getty example is notable particularly for the liquid brilliance of its colours which almost anticipate the vivid mother-of-pearl effects of Rubens' later works. The fusion of sensuous beauty with religious fervour attempted here for the first time in western art, found its most striking fulfillment in Bernini's *St Theresa.* (The contrast between the secular attractiveness of St Magdalen and her abject repentance and mortification is made more telling in the other versions by the presence of a skull supporting her prayerbook; X-rays recently taken show no trace of such a skull in the Getty version.)

Titian's subtle colour values form a vivid contrast to the broad and impetuous brushwork of Tintoretto's decorative paintings as seen in the *Toilet of Venus* and the *Allegory of Vanity*. A woman looking into a mirror is the central theme of both canvases, but the beholder is permitted to share in the mirror-reflexion only in the first one of the two. Venus' narcissistic self-admiration is shared by the attending servant, who, fascinated, interrupts her task of trimming her mistress's toe-nails. Both pictures are not only painted in a bold manner but also employ sweeping curvilinear accents aided by the exaggerated contrapposto-poses of the bodies.

The later Italian schools are represented only by two examples; Gentileschis' *Rest on the Flight into Egypt,* also one of several extant versions of what appears to have been a much admired composition, is closely allied to the *verismo* movement generally associated with Caravaggio. The biblical subject is now told in terms of common people, observed in their plain dress, and in their normal, unselfconscious behaviour. Thus the young Virgin nurses her sturdy infant with the quiet affection of any young Italian mother, while tired old Joseph has slumped backward to snatch some much needed sleep. The bare wall behind and the sharp illumination from the right stress the sculptural isolation of the figures, partially relieved by the harmony of the colours.

A magnificent portrait in full length of John Chetwynd, 1st Earl of Talbot, done in Rome in 1773 by the Roman academician Pompeo Batoni, is characteristic of the growing taste during that period for classical allusions. They appear not only in the various objects surrounding the young English Lord, but in his very pose which echoes a famous ancient sculpture of the youthful Meleagar.

Mr. Getty was fortunate indeed when he obtained for Sutton Place a large portrait attributed to Zuccaro and originally painted for this very house. It represents, in full length, Margaret Arundel, Lady Weston.

There are only two sixteenth-century Flemish paitings in the Getty collection, both of them portraits on a small scale. In one of them we see the sensitive face of a youth intently fixing the beholder with his eyes. He is dressed in black, and wears a flat red beret. It is a picture of high quality but its author is unknown. He must be looked for among the artists active in Antwerp between 1530–1540, judging by the style and the costume.

The second portrait, painted about half a century later, is historically of the greatest importance; it depicts the famous geographer Abraham Ortelius (1527–1598), one of the outstanding personalities of the Flemish Renaissance. The unknown artist in-

(continued page 108)

PAOLO VERONESE (1528–1588)

PORTRAIT OF A YOUNG MAN ▲

Venetian School

Canvas. Height: 19³/₄ ins. Width: 15³/₄ ins.

According to D. von Hadeln, this painting is a study for the *Young Man with a Greyhound,* formerly in the Havemeyer Collection and now in the Metropolitan Museum of Art, New York. According to information found at Brescia by M. Havemeyer, both are portraits of a member of the Colleoni family.

Collections: This painting was first in the Collection of Baron von Hadeln, Venice; Private Collection, Quebec; R. W. Redford. Acquired 1954.

Bibliography: Detlev Baron von HADELN, 'Some Portraits by Paolo Veronese', *Art In America,* XV, 1927, p. 251; L. VENTURI; *Italian Paintings In America,* 1933, III, pl. 569; Harry B. WEHLE, *The Metropolitan Museum of Art, A Catalogue of Italian, Spanish, and Byzantine Paintings,* New-York, 1940, p. 206; VALENTINER and WESCHER, op. cit., 1956, p. 20; B. BERENSON, *Italian Pictures of The Renaissance, Venetian School,* London, 1957, I, p. 136.

cluded a section of a globe showing countries bordering on the western Mediterranean, and a Latin motto *Contemno et Orno* (I despise and I honour). What lends a special significance to the work is the fact that it served as a model for Rubens when, in the 1630's he copied a series of famous men and women connected with the house of Plantin. Rubens' copy is in the Museum Plantin Mozetus at Antwerp where it has been believed to be based on a print. Rubens did not include the motto but otherwise followed the Getty picture faithfully except for his tendency to dramatize the expression.

The happy acquisition of Rubens' *Diana* gave to the Flemish seventeenth-century school in Mr Getty's collection a central focus around which may be grouped a number of large canvases showing the master's inspiration, if not always his own hand. The *Diana* which in the seventeenth century was in the famous collection of the Marquis de Léganès and still bears its inventory number, had disappeared from sight for a long time. There is no need to go into the stir it made when it was bought by Mr Getty and the vastly exaggerated controversy involving it and the Cleveland version. Enough to say that it is a superb picture, full of Rubens' vigour, movement, and sense of humour; its forceful and brilliant execution betrays the master's own hand in all essential details. It is the spontaneity of the brushwork that clearly distinguishes it from the handsome but more pedantically painted canvas in Cleveland. Its theme, as so often in Rubens' works, is the conflict between chastity and lust, and Rubens, not unexpectedly, is less than enthusiastic about chastity. The vigorously lunging satyr at the left is only weakly repelled by the nymph whom he tries to embrace, and the two nymphs at the right seem to consider the whole episode with equanimity if not some slight amusement. Diana, moving forward as she pets a huge affectionate hound, turns her back on the scene and appears to be entirely unconcerned. The relative isolation of individual figures and groups is a sign of a comparatively early date. The picture was probably painted around 1615.

If the *Diana* shows Ruben's art in a light-hearted vein, his ability to render emotion and pathos may be studied in the *Death of Dido*. Although the example from the Beistegui Collection in the Louvre appears to me the superior version of the two known ones, the Getty canvas is still a stirring work, deriving its impact from the tragic contrast between the physical beauty of the Queen of Carthage and the mental suffering that drives her to suicide.

(continued page 113)

PAOLO VERONESE (1528–1588)

SELF-PORTRAIT ▸

Canvas. Height: 76 ins. Width: 53 ins.

Several self-portraits of Veronese are known: Ridolphi mentions one belonging to the heirs of the Caliaris, another is found in the inventory of the collections of the emperor Rudolph. This one, aquired in Verona in 1802 by Lord Prior for the sum of 500 Napoleonic francs in gold, shows the artist full length, in an architectural setting, dressed in velvet, wearing a sword and holding a cap in his hand.

Collections: Count Salvi-Pindemonte-Moscardo, Verona; Cesare Bernasconi; Lord Prior; Hermann Goering.

Exhibitions: National Gallery, London, 1965.

Bibliography: Pietro CALIARI: 'Paolo Veroneses, sua vita e sue opere', Roma, 1888, pp. 222–23. Reproduced. Bernard BERENSON 'Italian Pictures of the Renaissance: Venetian School', London, 1957. Quoted vol. I. p. 138. Pl. 1042, vol. II. E. TIETZE-CONRAT: 'Paolo Veronese armato' (Ridolfi, II, 225). *Arte Veneta*, XIII–XIV, 1959–60, pp. 97–98.

PETER PAUL RUBENS (1577–1640)

DIANA AND HER NYMPHS DEPARTING ▶ FOR THE HUNT

Canvas. Height: 92½ ins. Width: 72 ins.

The painting of Diana, Nymphs and Satyrs is probably one of the earliest versions of this theme in Rubens' œuvre. The composition must have been much admired since it was repeated at least twice. A very good workshop replica, painted possibly with Rubens' assistance, is in the Museum of Art in Cleveland. It differs from the Getty version mainly in being more elaborate in marginal details. Another version in the museum in Kassel follows the painting in the Getty collection more faithfully but is much inferior in quality to both the Getty and the Cleveland versions.

Collections: Marquis de Leganès, described in the inventory of 1655 under No. 214; Duke of Altamira (traditionally); Duke of Salamanca (traditionally); The Roblot Family, Paris, about 1870–1951: Jean Neger, Geneva. Acquired 1961.

Exhibitions: Le Siècle de Rubens, Musées Royaux des Beaux-Arts de Belgique. Brussels. 15th Oct.–12th Dec. 1965.

Bibliography: Bulletin – Rubens, Antwerp, V, 1897, p. 169. (The Leganès description is found reproduced on this page, and is as follows:

> *Una pintura de Diana, de mano de Rubens, con 3 ninfas y la una la tiene asida un satiro de los brazos, y una vieja y 3 perros y la diosa con un venablo en la mano; de 2 varas de anco y 3 de alto.* (1 Vara equals 2.78 feet.)

There is no doubt that the description in the Leganès inventory refers to this composition despite the fact that the figure at the left, of which only the head is visible, was mistakenly identified as belonging to an old woman.)

PETER PAUL RUBENS (1577–1640)

THE DEATH OF DIDO ▲

Painted c. 1635–1638

Canvas. Height: 71 5/8 ins. Width: 48 1/2 ins.

According to Virgil, Dido killed herself when Aeneas abandoned her. Another story tells that in order to escape marriage with the King of Libya she stabbed herself on a funeral pyre erected under the pretence of soothing the Manès of her murdered husband. Another version of this work was to be found in the former collection of Carlos de Beistegui, and is now in the Louvre (No. RS 1942, 33).

Collections: A painting of Dido is listed in the inventory of Rubens' estate at his death in 1640, following number 174; Viscount Middleton, July, 31, 1851, and again 1852; Henry Farrer, 1866; Alan Beeton; obtained by Agnew, London, 1949. Acquired March, 1955.

Exhibitions: 'Works of Rubens', Wildenstein Galleries, New York, 1951, No. 33; 'Autumn Exhibition of Fine Pictures by Old Masters', Agnew's, London, Oct.–Dec., 1951, No. 30; Musée des Arts Décoratifs, Paris, 1954, No. 42.

Bibliography: John SMITH, *A Catalogue Raisonné of the Works of the Most Eminent Dutch, Flemish and French Painters,* London, 1830, II, p. 34, No. 175; G. REDFORD, *Art Sales,* London, 1888, I, p. 146, and II, p. 321; Max ROOSES, *L'Œuvre de P.P. Rubens,* Antwerp, 1890, III, p. 87; Ludwig BURCHARD, ed., Catalogue of 'A Loan Exhibition of Rubens at Wildenstein', New York, 20 Feb.–31 March 1951, p. 27; Catalogue, 'Chefs-d'Œuvre de la Curiosité du Monde', *Connaissance des Arts,* No. XXXVIII, 15 June 1954, p. 48; 'Notable Works of Art on the Market, Including Some at Present on Show at the Exhibition "Chefs-d'Œuvre de la Curiosité du monde" At The Musée des Arts Décoratifs, Paris', *Burlington Magazine,* XCVI, July, 1954, following p. 229; VALENTINER and WESCHER, op. cit., 1956, p. 21. For the C. de BEISTEGUI picture (now in the Louvre) *P. P. Rubens, Les Classiques de l'Art,* Paris, 1912, p. 395.

Among other paintings reflecting Rubens' style I should like to single out a large canvas with a young woman standing near an elaborate and succulent still life, probably painted by Snyders; Rubens had made a sketch for the whole composition and a special drawing for the female figure itself. The figure in the finished canvas appear to be the work of Jan Boeckhorst.

Mr. Getty's collection of Dutch paintings is dominated by two works of Rembrandt's. One, the *Portrait of Marten Looten* is among his earliest purchases; the other, the *St Bartholomew*, is his most recent. Painted by the youthful Rembrandt in the year in which he also finished the *Anatomy of Dr Tulp*, the *Marten Looten* was done with the same precision and in the same sparing range of colours that characterizes the famous portrayal of the Amsterdam physicians. It is also, quite literally, a 'speaking' likeness of the prosperous merchant. His lips seem to be parted, his forehead and eyebrows contracted as he intently looks at the beholder. While his right hand is placed at his chest as if to asseverate his regard and affection, his left hand holds the letter signed by Rembrandt and the crumpled envelope in which it appears to have come.

(continued page 116)

FRANS SNYDERS (1579–1657) and JAN BOECKHORST (1605–1668)

THE PANTRY ▲

Canvas. Height: 60½ ins. Width: 94½ ins.

A young woman carrying a tray comes towards her son sitting on a long table covered with various kinds of fruit, vegetables and poultry.

Collections: Peter William Baker, Ranston, about 1779; Maj. & Mrs. W. H. Gibson-Fleming; Sale Sotheby's 23 May 1960.

Bibliography: Sales Catalogue, London 23. 3. 1960, n° 44, Fred A. von BRAAM: 'World Collectors Annuary' 1960, vol. XII, n° 4.890, p. 433. G. Glück, 'Rubens, van Dyck, und ihr Kreis', Vienna 1933, p. 178 ff. reproduces two other versions of this composition.

NICOLAES ELIASZ, CALLED PICKENOY (AMSTERDAM, c. 1590–1653/6)

PORTRAIT OF A WOMAN ▲

Panel. Height: 46½ ins. Width: 34¼ ins.

Dutch School; Inscribed: AETATIS SUAE 21, ANº 1632

An unknown young woman, obviously belonging to the Dutch bourgeoisie at the beginning of the 17th Century, is shown here in a three-quarter pose, wearing a black dress with a gold-embroidered bodice and a collar with braided piping.

Collections: E. M. Denny, London, 1906; Louis Raphael, London (sold 20 May 1927, No. 17); A. W. Mensing, Amsterdam (sold 15 Nov. 1938, No. 82). Acquired November, 1938.

Exhibitions: Dutch Art, Royal Academy, London, 1929, No. 75; Rijksmuseum, Amsterdam, 1929, No. 47.

Bibliography: Burlington Magazine, I June 1904, p. 319 (Unsigned Editorial); Catalogue, 'Exhibition of Dutch Art, Royal Academy', London, 1930, 4 ed., p. 87; LE VANE and GETTY, op. cit., pp. 16 and 62; VALENTINER and WESCHER, op. cit., 1956, p. 22.

JACOB DUCK (c. 1600–1660)

THE REST OF THE SOLDIERS ▶

Panel. Height: 17 ins. Width: 24$^{3}/_{8}$ ins.

Dutch School, signed

In a vaulted hall with a central arcade, two soldiers are seated, one seen in profile, the other full face; they are smoking, drinking and chatting with a young woman seated on the steps. Their arms and equipment lie in the foreground. The painter's signature is on the overturned object at the right. This painting was engraved by Glairon-Mondet with the title 'The Flemish Conversation'.

Collections: Choiseul-Praslin (Sold 18 Feb. 1793, No. 114); Count Greffulhe; Adolphe Schloss, Paris (Sold 5 Dec. 1951), No. 18. Acquired December 1951.

Bibliography: Alfred von WURZBACH, *Niederländisches Künstler Lexikon,* 1906, I, p. 434; *Catalogue of the Schloss Sale, Galerie Charpentier,* Paris, 5 Dec. 1951, No. 18; *World Collectors Annuary,* Fred A. Van BRAAM, ed., Amsterdam, 1951, III, p. 190, No. 1139; VALENTINER and WESCHER, op. cit., 1956, p. 22. (There exists another painting by Duck in Utrecht with the same interior, but with different figures. See: *Catalogue of Paintings, Centraal Museum,* Utrecht, 1952, fig. 90.)

JOOS VAN CRAESBEEK (c. 1605–c. 1661)

THE CARDSHARPERS ▶

Panel. Height: 13$^{1}/_{2}$ ins. Width: 15$^{3}/_{8}$ ins.

Flemish School, about 1645, signed lower right, with interlaced monogram IVC

A man and a woman are playing cards. Behind the man, an accomplice holds a mirror which reveals to the woman her partner's hand. At the right, another woman is drinking and smoking and beside her stands a peasant looking at the wall. In the foreground is a seated child wearing a kind of turban and playing.

Collections: Princess Woronzoff, Adolphe Schloss (Sold at Paris, 5 Dec. 1951, No. 12). Acquired 5 Dec. 1951.

Exhibitions: 'Peinture Flamande; Rubens et Son Temps', Musée de l'Orangerie, Paris, 1936, No. 19.

Bibliography: Charles STERLING, 'Rubens et son temps', catalogue of the exhibition at the Musée de l'Orangerie, Paris, 1936, pp. 37–8; Catalogue, 'Adolphe Schloss Sale', Paris, 1951, No. 12; *World Collectors Annuary,* Fred A. van BRAAM, ed., Amsterdam, 1951, III, p. 163, No. 886; VALENTINER and WESCHER, op. cit., 1956, p. 23.

One needs only to compare this portrait with the one of a Lady by Nicolaes Eliasz (Pickenoy), painted in the very same year, to appreciate why in the 1630's Rembrandt swept before him all the established Amsterdam portrait painters. Taken by itself, Eliasz' picture is a charming work, notable particularly for the perfect rendering of lace-work, embroideries, jewellery, and the large neatly pleated collar. Yet where Rembrandt's model is aglow with life and individual character, Eliasz' young lady is frozen into an impersonal image of middle class respectability.

The recent acquisition of the *St. Bartholomew* has added to the numerical preponderance of Dutch painting the weight of a universally acclaimed masterpiece. Popularized in mezzotint as early as the mid-eighteenth century, the picture was exhibited several times and has been included in all standard works of Rembrandt's paintings. Yet it is still a problem why Rembrandt around 1660–1661 planned a series of Apostles (a series never completed, so it seems). The subject was common in Catholic countries but hardly ever treated in Calvinist Holland. Rembrandt's treatment of the theme, at any rate, differs greatly from that of Rubens or van Dyck. The Saints of the Flemish painters were figures marked by their divine mission; in the selection and the posing of their models these artists were guided by the desire to portray them as chosen men, ennobled by their spiritual function. No such idealization is found in Rembrandt's apostles. St Bartholomew in Mr Getty's picture can be identified only because of the conspicuous presence of his attribute, the knife, the instrument of his martyrdom. In the past, this resulted in grotesque misinterpretations. The picture has been known under the titles *The Assassin* and *Rembrandt's Cook.*

(continued page 118)

REMBRANDT VAN RIJN (1606–1669)

PORTRAIT OF MARTEN LOOTEN ►

Signed with monogram R. H. L., dated Jan. 1632 *Panel. Height: 36½ ins. Width: 30 ins.*

This portrait of a wealthy Amsterdam businessman was painted around 1632. It is probably the second portrait commissioned from Rembrandt. In this half-length portrait, the subject is seen in a three-quarter pose, looking towards the spectator. He is dressed in a dark cape and wears a wide-brimmed felt hat. In his hand he holds a letter bearing the inscription 'MARTEN LOOTEN, XI JANUARIS 1632' followed by four lines of writing the deciphering of which has been the basis of polemics among Dutch specialists.

Collections: Cardinal Fesch, Rome (Sold at Rome, 17 March 1845, No. 190); William Coningham (Sold at London, 25 April 1849); Sir George Lindsay Holford, Dorchester House, London (Sold at Christie's, 17 May 1928, No. 34); Anton W. MENSING (Sold in Amsterdam, 15 Nov. 1938, No. 86). Acquired 15 November 1938.

Exhibitions: British Institution, London, 1851 and 1862, No. 13; Royal Academy, London, 1887, No. 93; Rembrandt Tentoonstellung, Amsterdam, 1898, No. 20; Royal Academy, London, 1899, No. 63; Exhibition of Dutch Art, Royal Academy, London, 1929, No. 150; Rijksmuseum, Amsterdam, 1929, No.112; Boymans Museum, Rotterdam, 1938, No. 126; 'Masterpieces of Art', New York World's Fair, 1939, No. 296; Chicago Art Institute; 'Frans Hals, Rembrandt', Los Angeles County Museum, Los Angeles, 1947, No. VI; 'Rembrandt Exhibition', Wildenstein, New York, 1950, No. 5.

Bibliography: Gustave WAAGEN, *Art Treasures In Great Britain,* 1854, II, 200; C. VOSMAER, *Rembrandt,* Paris, 1877, pp. 114 and 495; E. DUTUIT, *Tableaux et Dessins de Rembrandt,* Paris, 1885, pp. 45 and 66; E. MICHEL, *Rembrandt,* New York, 1894, I, p. 117, and, II, p. 236; E. W. MOES, *Inconographia Batava,* Amsterdam, 1897, II, p. 38, No. 4639; Wilhelm BODE and Hofstede DE GROOT, *Rembrandt,* Paris, 1897, II, p. 26, No. 72; W. R. VALENTINER, 'Rembrandt', *Klassiker der Kunst,* Stuttgart-Leipzig, 1909, I, p. 77; Hofstede DE GROOT, *Beschreibendes und Kritisches Verzeichnis der Werke der Hervorragendsten Holländischen Maler des XVII Jahrhunderts,* Esslingen-Paris, 1915, VI, p. 314, No. 659; D. S. MELDRUM, *Rembrandt's Paintings,* London, 1923, p. 188, No. 69; Werner WEISBACH, *Rembrandt,* Berlin, 1926, p. 264; Catalogue, *Dutch Exhibition, Royal Academy,* London, 1929, p. 108, No. 150; *The Paintings of Rembrandt,* A. BREDIUS, ed., Vienna, 1936, No. 166; *Catalogue of European Paintings, New York World's Fair,* W. R. VALENTINER, ed., 1939, pp. 144–5, No. 296; LE VANE and GETTY, op. cit., pp. 13–52.

The real reason for these errors of interpretation, obviously, was not the presence of the knife as such. It is found in Rembrandt's use of a model who lost none of his simple humanity in his transfer to the artist's canvas. He has the short hair and moustache, the heavily lined forehead and baggy eyes, the gnarled leathery hands of a very common man. His expression has none of the devotion, the piety, or the exaltation commonly stressed in Flemish, Italian, or Spanish paintings of saints. Rather he seems to be caught in a very human dilemma that renders him pensive, perhaps even a little perplexed. And yet, this is more than the portrait of a Dutchman in a quandary. A huge man with massive shoulders and powerful hands, he is also a sensitive, complex, and deeply responsible being who seems to be listening for an inner voice answering troublesome questions. At the same time, he fixes the beholder with his intense glance as if to indicate that his problems are ours as well.

Instead of using the smooth finish of the *Marten Looten,* Rembrandt painted *St Bartholomew* with bold, rapid strokes that make the picture look strangely modern but primarily succeed in conveying the impression of a restless emotional activity. As so often in Rembrandt's late works, the light seems to come from within. While not exactly looking like a saint, the man rendered in the role of St Bartholomew indeed appears like one truly and divinely illuminated.

None of Rembrandt's pupils ever achieved the distinction of the master, though several were worthy of the historian's attention. One of them, Aert de Gelder, is represented in Mr. Getty's collection with a beautiful and tender interpretation of *David Receiving the Sword of Goliath from Ahimelech.* Yet is impossible here to do justice to every one of the many fine seventeenth-century Dutch pictures that occupy such a large place in Mr. Getty's collection. There are characteristic landscapes by Jan van Goyen, S. Ruysdael, A. van der Croos, F. Moucheron, A. Cuyp, and Jan van der Heyden, most of them signed and dated. The Cuyp has the additional interest of containing the portrait of what looks like a prosperous Dutch merchant supervising the crating of goods about to be shipped abroad.

Two paintings in this group deserve special mention. Both were done by unusually gifted artists who died very young. P. Potter who died at the age of twenty-eight painted the *Cavalier near an Inn* when he was only twenty-five. It is a small panel, done in a crisp and cool style and with a keen eye for special light effects. A. van de Velde who died at thirty-five was only twenty-eight when he painted what at first glance looks like a landscape with animals and shepherds. Actually, its peaceful bucolic air is deceptive; it renders the moment when Mercury, keeping a careful eye on his victim, draws the sword to cut off the head of sleeping Argus. The placid white heifer at the left is Io, transformed into bovine shape by Hera's jealousy. The artist prepared the canvas in a beautiful drawing (now at the Teyler Museum at Haarlem) but Io's truly radiant prominence was realized only in the painting.

The leisurely life of the seventeenth-century Dutch, glimpsed in most landscapes, is depicted more fully in the many *genre* paintings in the collection.

At their staid best they appear in Cornelis de Mans' family group. The members of a well-to-do family have evidently finished a Sunday breakfast. Now they are getting ready to go to church. The rather forbidding mother is handing a prayer-book to the younger of the boys, and the little girl holds the freshly starched cap she will wear modestly on top of the dainty one that already adorns her hair. Few pictures have caught equally well the spirit of honest, if somewhat dull uprightness that somehow seems typical of Dutch seventeenth-century Calvinism.

(continued page 124)

REMBRANDT VAN RIJN (1606–1669)

SAINT BARTHOLOMEW ▲

Signed and dated, lower right, Rembrandt/f. 1661 *Canvas. Height: 34 1/8 ins. Width: 29 1/2 ins.*

Collections: John Blackwood Collection, London, 1757 (but not in the Blackwood Sale, 1778, as Hofstede de Groot states); Perhaps in the Prince Trivulzio Sale, Amsterdam, 29 August 1764, No. 109, and anonymous sale, Amsterdam, 30 November 1772, No. 137; Almost certainly acquired by Richard Payne Knight of Downton Castle, then to Andrew Rouse Boughton Knight, Downton Castle; Major W. M. P. Kincaid Lennox, Downton Castle (Sold at Sotheby's 27 June 1962, No. 10). Acquired June, 1962.

Exhibitions: Royal Academy, Winter Exhibition, London, 1882, No. 234; Royal Academy, Winter Exhibition, 1899, No. 99; Royal Academy, Winter Exhibition, 1912, No. 52; Royal Academy, 'Dutch Art Exhibition', 1929, No. 86; Birmingham Art Gallery, 'Art Treasures of the Midlands', 1934, No. 152; Rijksmuseum, Amsterdam, and Boymans Museum, Rotterdam, 'Rembrandt Exhibition', 1956, No. 87.

Bibliography: John SMITH, *A Catalogue Raisonné of The Works Of The Most Eminent Dutch, Flemish, and French Painters,* London, 1836, VII, No. 359; C. VOSMAER, *Rembrandt,* Paris, 1877, pp. 361 and 562; E. DUTUIT, *Tableaux et Dessins de Rembrandt,* Paris, 1885, p. 43, No. 434; Emile MICHEL, *Rembrandt,* New York, 1894, II, p. 236; W. BODE and Hofstede DE GROOT, Rembrandt, 1897–1906, VII, p. 82, No. 508; Jan VETH, *Rembrandt's Leven en Kunst,* Amsterdam, 1906, pp. 112 and 130; Hofstede DE GROOT, *Beschreibendes und Kritisches Verzeichnis der Werke der Hervorragendsten Holländischen Maler des XVII Jahrhunderts,* Esslingen–Paris, 1915, VI, p. 98, No. 168; W. R. VALENTINER, *Rembrandt, Klassiker der Kunst,* I, 1909, p. 456; W. R. VALENTINER, *Kunstchronik und Kunstmarkt,* XXXII, 1920–1, pp. 221 f; J. CHARRINGTON, *Catalogue of the Mezzotints After Rembrandt,* 1923, Nos. 82 and 130; A. BREDIUS, *The Paintings of Rembrandt,* 1937, fig. 615; H. FOCILLON and L. GOLDSCHEIDER, *Rembrandt,* 1960, pl. 108.

ANTHONIE DE LORME (About 1610–1673)

INTERIOR OF CHURCH OF ST LAWRENCE AT ROTTERDAM ▲

Dutch School, signed and dated, lower left, 1662 *Canvas. Height: 24 3/4 ins. Width: 18 1/2 ins.*

A transversal view, from the choir, of the centre of the nave, supported by pillars and flanked in the background by two high ogival windows. Two peasants seen from the back, an elegant woman and her greyhound, painted by L. de Jongh as are the other figures, enliven the foreground. This theme recurs frequently in the work of De Lorme, of whom Monsieur de Monconys, one of his contemporaries, said: 'He only paints views of the Rotterdam church, but he does them well.' Another version dated the same year is in the Hermitage in Leningrad.

Collections: Forbes Robertson, London; Adolphe Schloss, Paris (Sold at Paris, 5 Dec. 1951, No. 34). Acquired 5 Dec. 1951. VALENTINER and WESCHER, op. cit., 1956, p. 23.

Bibliography: H. JANTZEN, *Das Niederländische Architekturbild,* Leipzig, 1910, p. 77; Catalogue, 'Adolphe Schloss Sale', Paris, 1951, No. 34, pl. XXXIII; *World Collectors Annuary,* Fred A. van BRAAM, ed., Amsterdam, 1951, III, p. 325, No. 2518; VALENTINER and WESCHER, op. cit., 1956, p. 23.

CORNELIS DE MAN (1621–1706)

THE FAMILY MEAL ▲

Dutch School

Canvas. Height: 22 7/8 ins. Width: 28 3/8 ins.

In a comfortable but plain room, five people finish their meal seated around a table. At the left, the master of the house can be identified by his red and gold skull-cap. After having been attributed for many years to Brekelenkam, a pupil of Gerard Dou, by Alfassa and Bredius, this painting was re-attributed to its rightful author by Mme Cl. Brière-Misme.

Collections: Adolphe Schloss, Paris (Sold 5 Dec. 1951, No. 36). Acquired 5 Dec. 1951.

Exhibitions: 'Tri-centenaire de Rembrandt', Leyden, 1906, No. 5 (As by Brekelenkam); Los Angeles County Museum, 1952.

Bibliography: Paul ALFASSA, 'Le Tri-centenaire de Rembrandt à Leyde', *Revue de l'Art Ancien et Moderne,* XX, 1906, p. 200; A. BREDIUS, *De Leidsche Tentoonstelling In 1906,* Haarlem, 1907, No. 15; C. BRIÈRE-MISME, 'Un émule de Vermeer et de Pieter de Hooch, Cornelis de Man, I', *Oud Holland,* LII, 1935, p. 23; Catalogue, 'Adolphe Schloss Sale', Paris, 1951, No. 36, pl. XXV; *World Collectors Annuary,* Fred A. van BRAAM, ed., Amsterdam, 1951, III, p. 336, No. 2630; VALENTINER and WESCHER, op. cit., 1956, p. 22.

WILLEM KALF (1622–1693)

STILL LIFE ▲

Dutch School, signed KALF

Canvas. Height: 41 ins. Width: 32¹/₄ ins.

Willem Kalf, although he painted landscapes and interiors, is especially known for his still-life painting. He lived for several years in Paris, and it is probably towards the end of his visit that he painted this canvas, which already shows the simplified style which he adopted during his career in Amsterdam.

Collections: Georg Krakau, Berlin; A.W. Mensing, Amsterdam. Acquired at the Mensing Sale, 15 November 1938, No. 51.

Exhibitions: Madrid, 1921, No. 46; Copenhagen, 1922, No. 63; Nederlandsche stillevens uit 5 eeuwen, The Hague, 1926.

Bibliography: '*Catalogue des Tableaux Anciens*', Collection of W. M. MENSING, Amsterdam, 1938, p. 14, No. 51; VALENTINER and WESCHER, op. cit., 1954, p. 16; LE VANE and Getty, op cit., pp. 16 and 62; Ingvar BERGSTRÖM, *Dutch Still Life Painting In The Seventeenth Century*, London, 1956, p. 278, fig. 226.

JACOB VREL (Active, Delft, About 1634–62)

STREET OF A DUTCH TOWN ▲

Dutch School, signed

Panel. Height: 16 1/8 ins. Width: 13 3/4 ins.

A street view. On either side, red-brick houses typical of Dutch towns. In the foreground, left, a baker's stall; in the background, a strolling merchant. The painting was attributed to Vermeer during the 19th Century.

Collections: Thoré-Bürger (Sold at Paris, 5 Dec. 1892), No. 33; Adolphe Schloss, Paris (Sold 5 Dec. 1951, No. 60). Acquired 5 Dec. 1951.

Exhibitions: Rétrospective du Palais des Champs-Elysées, Paris, June 1866, No. 112 (As by Vermeer, and bearing signature VMEER).

Bibliography: W. BÜRGER, 'Van der Meer de Delft', *Gazette des Beaux Arts,* XXI, 1866, pp. 569–70, No. 54; Hofstede DE GROOT, 'Die Auction Thoré-Bürger', *Repertorium für Kunstwissenschaft,* XVI, 1893, p. 116; Clotilde BRIÈRE-MISME, 'Un Intimiste Hollandais: Jacob Vrel', *Revue de L'Art Ancien et Moderne,* LXVIII, 1935, p. 109; Germain BAZIN, *'Les grands maîtres hollandais',* Paris, 1950, p. 187, No. 115; Catalogue 'Adolphe Schloss Sale', Paris, 1951, No. 60; *World Collectors Annuary,* 1951, III, p. 514, No. 4345; VALENTINER and WESCHER, op. cit., 1956, p. 23.

The interior of a Dutch church is the subject of a picture of 1662 by the fairly rare Antonis de Lorme. Utterly simple in its symmetrical composition, and sparing in details, it nevertheless attains a poetic quality owing to the subtle purity of its colours and the soaring beauty of the gothic architecture. Among the visitors to the church we notice an elegant lady with a greyhound, followed, at a respectful distance, by a man servant, and–in a delightful contrast–a stocky young couple in fisherfolk's garb, seen from behind, the man's arm curving familiarly around the girl's waist. They look, appropriately, at the tablet listing the 107th psalm–the psalm of all sea-going people.

A very different social milieu is hinted at in Jacob Duck's picture of a girl with two soldiers. The Dutch held soldiers in low esteem, and the two men in this panel are indeed hardly paragons of virtue. Besides, with their gear, they have come with booty to this room below street level. Some trinkets have found the way to the girl's lap (possibly with the aid of the pair of dice placed so conspicuously in the foreground). Both men look at the girl expectantly, as if waiting to see who will be favoured first.

While overtly, at least, the behaviour of the characters in Duck's picture stays within the bounds of propriety, no matter what their true aim, the figures in Joos van Craesbeck's painting are definitely undignified, if not downright crooked. Craesbeck was actually Flemish, but as a follower of Brouwer he reflected tendencies of Dutch painting. The central action of the work is a variation on the theme of card-sharps, made popular by Caravaggio. The woman at the left makes her decision what card to play by conveniently examining the 'hand' of her partner in a mirror held up behind his back by her accomplice. The disorderliness of the milieu is also characterized by a large woman who drinks as well as smokes, and, further back, by a man who did not go very far to relieve himself.

The high accomplishments of Dutch still-life are represented in an early canvas by Willem Kalf, perhaps from his Paris period and foreshadowing appropriately enough the still-lifes of Chardin. Without the deep richness of colour of Kalf's later works, it has many delicious details such as the reflection in the silver tankard of the glass with red wine. It also does full justice to the exquisite craftsmanship that shaped the golden pitcher, the central object of the stately composition.

Vrel's little scene comes last, but not least; it is not surprising that it once was attributed to Vermeer. Vermeer probably knew the modest street scenes by this obscure painter and remembered them when he did his *Little Street*, now in the Rijksmuseum

(continued page 130)

HYACINTHE RIGAUD (1659–1743)

LOUIS XIV ▸

Painted in 1704

Canvas. Height: 114 ins. Width: 64 ins.

The Sun-King is shown in his coronation robes, the crown resting on a cushion at his side. Two other copies of this painting can be found in the Louvre and the Château de Versailles, respectively. All three were painted in 1704 after the original of 1701. In America, this painting is known as La Belle Jambe.

Collections: Remained at the Tuileries Palace until the French Revolution; Don Jaime, direct descendant of Louis XIV. When he died in Frohsdorf, Austria, his daughter sold it (Sotheby's, 20 July 1938). Acquired 1938.

Bibliography: Catalogue of the Celebrated Pictures and Drawings of the Collection of the Royal House of France Removed From Schloss Frohsdorf, London, 1938, p. 25, No. 136; LE VANE and GETTY, op. cit., pp. 62–3, 143–4, 159–61.

LOUIS MOREAU THE ELDER (1740–1806)

◄ THE SQUARE LOUIS XV IN PARIS

Canvas. Height: 19 5/8 ins. Width: 29 1/2 ins.

Painted about 1790

A view of the Place Louis XV, now the Place de la Concorde, in Paris, slightly before 1790, at which time the construction of the bridge was undertaken. In the centre, the equestrian statue of Louis XV by Bouchardon, which was destroyed in 1792; in the background, the two buildings of Gabriel: at that time the building on the right was the royal garde-meuble; on the right is the entrance to the Tuileries.

Collection: Rodolphe Kann, Paris. Acquired October, 1957 at Pardo Gallery, Paris.

Bibliography: P. WESCHER, 'The Place Louis XV by Louis Moreau The Elder', *Bulletin of the J. Paul Getty Museum of Art,* Malibu, I, 1957, pp. 26–29, fig. II.

THOMAS GAINSBOROUGH (1727–1788)

PORTRAIT OF JAMES A. CHRISTIE (1730–1803) ▲

Painted in 1778

Canvas. Height: 49 1/2 ins. Width: 39 3/8 ins.

This is a portrait of the founder of the famous London auction gallery Christie, Manson and Woods, which had been in existence for twelve years when the picture was painted.

Collections: Christie family until 1927 (Sold 20 May 1927 at London, Lot No. 29, purchased by Agnew). Acquired July, 1938 from Colnaghi.

Exhibitions: Royal Academy, London, 1778, No. 117; 1817, No. 137; 1859, No. 94; National Portrait Exhibition, South Kensington, 1867, No. 793; Old Masters Exhibition, Burlington House, 1891, No. 4; Ipswich, England, 1927. No. 52; 'Gainsborough Exhibition' Cincinnati, 1931, No. 2; 'Tentoonstelling van Oude Kunst', Rijksmuseum, Amsterdam, 1936, No. 51; New York World's Fair, New York, 1939, No. 130.

Bibliography: George FULCHER, *Life of Thomas Gainsborough*, London, 1856; William ROBERTS, *Memorials of Christie's*, London, 1897; Walter ARMSTRONG, *Gainsborough*, London 1898; Mortimer MENPES and James GREIG, *Gainsborough*, London, 1909; Catalogue, 'Bicentenary Memorial Exhibition of the Works of T. Gainsborough', Ipswich Museum, 1927; William T. WHITLEY, *Art in England 1800–1820*, Cambridge, 1928; Catalogue, Gainsborough Exhibition, Cincinnati, 1931; 'Tentoonstelling van Oude Kunst', Rijksmuseum, Amsterdam, 1936; Catalogue of European Paintings, New York World's Fair VALENTINER, ed., 1939; LE VANE and GETTY; VALENTINER and WESCHER, 1956; Ellis WATERHOUSE, *Gainsborough*, London, 1958.

THOMAS GAINSBOROUGH (1727–1788)

PORTRAIT OF ANNE, COUNTESS OF CHESTERFIELD ▲

Painted about 1778

Canvas. Height: 86 ins. Width: 61 ins.

The daughter of Reverend Thistlethwayte, Anne married Philip Stanhope, fifth Earl of Chesterfield, in 1777. She is shown seated, leaning against a pedestal and dressed in blue silk with a brown and gold shawl.

Collections: Passed to the Countess of Carnarvon, 1871; Earl of Carnarvon, Highclere Castle, Newbury (Sold 22 May 1925, No. 108); Sir John Leigh, Bt. Acquired at Sotheby's 18 November 1959, Lot No. 38.

Exhibitions: Royal Academy, London, 1778, No. 113; Burlington House, Winter Exhibition, 1887, No. 146.

Bibliography: Walter ARMSTRONG, *Gainsborough*, London, 1898, p. 193; M. MENPES and J. GREIG, *Gainsborough*, London, 1909, p. 128; Ellis WATERHOUSE, *Gainsborough*, London, 1958, p. 59, No. 141; *World Collectors Annuary*, Fred A. van BRAAM, ed., Amsterdam, 1959, XI, p. 149, No. 1620.

in Amsterdam. His painting is more monumental than anything by Vrel, but it was Vrel who had discovered the special charm of cobble-stones, humble brick houses, scattered patches of plaster, irregular groups of windows—and people for whom time means nothing.

The eighteenth century, so brilliantly represented in Mr. Getty's collection of applied art, can be studied in only a small group of paintings. Among them, however, is one of the really great English portraits, Gainsborough's *Portrait of James A. Christie.* Even if it were a less brilliant performance, it would deserve attention as the likeness of one of the first great auctioneers, the founder of a firm that is still among the leaders in the field. Yet it is also a marvel of characterization, bringing out clearly the suavity, shrewdness, and wit that obviously qualified Christie for his job. Dressed with elegant informality, relaxing casually against a picture frame, a half-smile on his lips, the auctioneer looks out with eyes that will notice and appraise the slightest move. Gainsborough included parts of two pictures in the composition. Of one we see only part of a sumptuously carved frame. The other, in a simple moulding, is a landscape probably invented by Gainsborough himself.

A second Gainsborough, the full-length *Portrait of the Countess of Chesterfield* shows the lady in a pensive mood, painted with the emotional reticence and sophisticated colouring that distinguish Gainsborough's portraits from those of Reynolds. Romney's *Duchess of Cumberland* by contrast, was done in Reynold's more expansive manner. Reynolds himself is represented by a charming portrait of Joanna Leigh, Mrs. R. B. Lloyd (later married to Peter Beckford), seen in a pose similar to her full-length portrait in the collection of Lord Rothschild. Moreau l'Ainé's historically interesting portrayal of the Place Louis XV (today Place de la Concorde) is the last painting of the eighteenth century, forming a French counterpart of the then popular Italian *vedute.*

Of the few later pictures I want at least to mention the poetically shimmering Monet, a rural scene full of sunlight by Pissaro, the unusually impressionistic early Gauguin and the strikingly composed Bonnard; impressive as these pictures are, they only serve to underscore the point that the centre of gravitation in Mr. Getty's collection of paintings lies definitely elsewhere.

If one asks—in retrospect—what quality stands out in this collection of paintings, it is perhaps best to point out its conservatism. No matter how daring Mr. Getty may have

(continued page 132)

GEORGE ROMNEY (1734–1802)

THE DUCHESS OF CUMBERLAND ▸

Painted in 1788

Canvas. Height: $53^1/_2$ *ins. Width:* $45^1/_4$ *ins.*

Anne, the daughter of Simon Lutrell, first married to Christopher Horton, married Henry Frederick, Duke of Cumberland and brother of George III in 1771. The precise notes found in the papers of George Romney enable us to date this painting in the spring of 1788. The painter notes that he received the sum of 50 guineas from his illustrious model for her portrait.

Collections: Lady Horton, Catton Hall, Derbyshire; Lord Wenlock, Escrick Park, Yorks; Knoedler and Co., New York; Elbert H. Gary, New York (Sold at American Art Association, New York, 20 April 1928, No. 36); Henry Walters (Sold at Parke-Bernet, April–May, 1941, No. 986). Acquired 1941.

Exhibitions: National Portrait Exhibition, London, 1867 (see E. H. Gary catalogue).

Bibliography: Rev. John ROMNEY, *Memoirs of The Life and Work of George Romney*, London, 1830, p. 199; George PASTON, *George Romney*, London, 1903, pp. 108 and 193; Humphry WARD and W. ROBERTS, *Romney*, London, 1904, II, p. 37; The Mrs Henry Walters Art Collection, New York, 1941, II, p. 296, No. 986; *American Art Annual*, XXV, 1928, p. 461; LE VANE and GETTY, op. cit., p. 162.

PIERRE AUGUSTE RENOIR (1841–1919)

THE VILLAGE OF ESSOYES ▲

Signed at the lower right

Canvas. Height: 10¼ ins. Width: 12⅝ ins.

Renoir often stayed in this village in the Aube, on the Ource river, the birthplace of his wife and his famous model, Gabrielle. He owned a house there where young painters came to visit him during the summer.

Acquired at the Charpentier Gallery, Sale of 12 March 1956, No. 76.

Bibliography: Ambroise VOLLARD, *Tableaux, Pastels, et Dessins de Pierre-Auguste Renoir,* Paris, 1918, II, pl. p. 110; Catalogue of the Sale of 12 March 1956, Paris, No. 76, pl. XX.

been in business affairs–a field which I am not qualified to judge–as a collector of painting he has rarely ventured into the unknown or the problematical. It is perhaps precisely for this very reason that his collection of paintings is so enjoyable. Without being superficial or trite, the paintings which he collected speak primarily to the senses. They entertain, and they delight. They were bought, one feels, because they were immediately appealing, not because they were challenging or 'important'. As a group they have preserved the pleasurable sensation that made each one desirable. When all is said and done, no better compliment can be paid to a collection than that it indicates as this one does, a genuine respect for, and a spontaneous awareness of beauty.

CLAUDE MONET (1840–1926)

THE CLIFFS OF POURVILLE IN THE MORNING ▶

Canvas. Height: 25¼ ins. Width: 39⅜ ins.

Signed and dated lower right, '97

The cliffs with red-tinted highlights, an arm of the sea, a scrap of beach, the scene bathed in a vaporous blue, these are the elements of this work painted by Monet near Dieppe shortly before beginning work on the Nymphéas. Signed and dated at the lower left: 97.

Collections: Bought by Durand-Ruel at MM. Bernheim-Jeune, 27 January 1899. Acquired at the Charpentier Gallery, 12 March 1956, No. 68.

Bibliography: 'Catalogue of the Sale of 12 March 1956', Paris, No. 68.

EDGAR DEGAS (1834–1917)

SEA-SIDE LANDSCAPE ▶

Canvas. Height: 19¾ ins. Width: 24 ins.

Pure landscapes are rarely to be found in Degas's work. In the beginning they served as a pretext for mythological scenes and later for horse-racing scenes. Between 1868 and 1880, however, there are some pastels and canvases inspired by the sea. The present example has the stamp of the Degas atelier on the stretcher.

Collections: Mlle. J. Fèvre (Sold 12 June 1934, at the Charpentier Gallery, No. 110). Acquired at the Charpentier Gallery 18 March 1959, No. 38.

Bibliography: 'Collection Lady Kent et Divers Amateurs', Paris, 1959, No. 38, pl. XVII; *World Collectors Annuary*, Fred A. Van BRAAM, ed., Amsterdam, 1959, IX, p. 101, No. 1090.

PAUL GAUGUIN (1848–1903)

LANDSCAPE NEAR ROUEN ▸

Canvas. Height: 22 ins. Width: 33¾ ins.

Signed and dated 'Rouen '84' in the lower right

Also the inscription 'A mon ami William Lund'.

Gauguin's landscapes which are not part of his Brittany period nor painted during his stay in Provence are extremely rare. The present example shows a curve of the Seine with grazing cows in the foreground and is dated Rouen, 1884.

Collections: William Lund; Fr. Sander (According to Catalogue of Gauguin Exhibition, 1948). Acquired at Sotheby's 6 May 1959, No. 129.

Exhibitions: 'Mit bedste Kunstvaerk', Statens Art Museum, 1941, No. 56; 'Paul Gauguin Exhibition', Ny Carlsberg Glyptotek, Copenhagen, May–June, 1948, No. 24.

Bibliography: *'Catalogue of Highly Important Impressionistic and Modern Paintings and Drawings'*, Sotheby's, 1959, p. 50, pl. 129; *World Collectors Annuary*, Fred A. van BRAAM, ed., Amsterdam, 1959, XI, p. 151, No. 1642.

Rouen
William Lund
Gauguin 84

EDGAR DEGAS (1834–1917)

◂ THREE DANCERS IN PINK

Canvas. Height: 39 3/8 ins. Width: 21 1/4 ins.

Painted about 1886

Three dancers against a green background. The first, in the foreground, is seen from the front and partially hides the second. The third, at the right, is seen in profile. Stamp at the lower right.

Collections: First Degas Sale, 16 May 1918, No. 60; Collection Danthon, Ed. Riche, Neuilly-sur-Seine. Acquired at the Charpentier Gallery 12 March 1956, No. 40.

Exhibitions: 'Works by Degas', Glasgow and London, 1928 (According to Lemoisne).

Bibliography: Atelier Degas, First Sale, 1918, p. 75, No. 60; J. B. MANSON, *Life and Work of Edgar Degas,* London, 1927, pl. 67; P. A. LEMOISNE, *Degas et son oeuvre,* Paris, 1946, III, p. 516, No. 885; Catalogue of the Sale of 12 March, 1956, Paris, No. 40, pl. XIII.

PIERRE BONNARD (1867–1947)

WOMAN IN THE NUDE ▶

Canvas. Height: 54½ ins. Width: 31½ ins.

Signed in the upper right

Three-quarter view of a model standing in front of a screen, looking down. A voluminous dressing-gown falls from her hand.

Collection: E. J. *Power,* London. Acquired at Sotheby's 6 July 1960, No. 130.

Bibliography: Catalogue of the Sale of 6 July 1960, London, p. 29, pl. 130; *Art Prices Current,* XXXVII, 1959–60, p. 224, No. 5729; *World Collectors Annuary,* Fred A. van BRAAM, ed., Amsterdam, 1960, XII, p. 38, No. 49.

FURNITURE AND OBJETS D'ART

by

PIERRE VERLET

[Chief Keeper of the Department of Furniture and Objets d'art]
[Louvre, Paris]

GERMAN CABINET

Height: 15 1/2 ins. Length: 21 1/2 ins. Depth: 16 ins.

Southern Germany – Late 16th century.

Portable bureau in marqueterie with lateral handles and metal corners. The marqueterie motifs on the lid are in relief: the table is surmounted by an hour-glass, an angel poised upon a scull. The drop-flap is decorated by a vase, and with carvings and ivy-leaves. The interior consists of ten drawers, adorned with grottos and scrolls. In the centre of the desk is a girl playing a guitar, with a background of antique ruins.

Coll. Catherine Schratt, Vienna; F. Steinmeyer, Lucerne.
Bibl. L. MÖLLER: Der Wrangelschrank und die verwandten Süddeutschen Intarsienmöbel des 16. Jahrhunderts, Berlin 1956, Deutscher Verein für Kunstwissenschaft.

Truth prevails sooner or later. Some famous collections, much admired in their period, end by giving an impression of sadness, mediocrity and false richness. Some modest art lovers who have not followed fashion because they have been on the sidelines have succeeded in assembling a select group of works of art chosen with so much taste and discernment that later on they become leaders. These two types of collector existed in the nineteenth century, and we find them today. It would be easy to name examples of both categories.

However, there is perhaps a third category: that of the rich collector who, by his choices, comes close to being the ideal art-lover. There are several of this type, and Jean Paul Getty, as a collector of eighteenth-century French furniture, is one of them. Friendship should not prejudice one. Like anyone else, he has sometimes regretted buying a certain piece of furniture. But despite this, and without devoting large sums of money and publicity to his collecting, he has succeeded in assembling in his Californian museum some of the most precious specimens of the work of the Parisian cabinet makers of the eighteenth century.

How can we explain this? By flair or good advisers? Flair is not something one takes on and off, and advisers flock around money. Fine furniture becomes increasingly hard to come by. It has to be sought out and discovered, and then held on to.

Nobody should be surprised to see one man collect a number of masterpieces, for flair grows through experience, planned or otherwise, and out of hard work, whether it be conscious or unconscious. Perhaps geniuses do exist, but one is more inclined to trust in the energy and intelligence of certain men who are–to be sure–gifted with a natural finesse, but who are above all devoted to the acquisition of knowledge. Whether it be gained from dealers, books, the family or in front of the objects themselves, their experience is their greatest asset, allowing them to hunt down the noblest and most unusual quarry with confidence. To come back to the word 'truth': here are a few examples of truly regal selections.

(continued page 145)

CHARLES CRESSENT (1685–1766)

WRITING TABLE ▲

Height: 31 ins. Length: 79 ins. Width: 35 ins.

Regency style rosewood desk, decorated on the sides with satyr heads; the corner *espagnolettes* are surmounted with a shell, the face surrounded by a garland. The drawers are outlined in straight moulding. These drawers are decorated with fauns' masks similar to those on the *fauteuil bateau* of Cressent in the Louvre. The middle drawer has a keyhole surmounted by a shell with leaves at the corners (similar to Cressent's commode in the Museum at Meaux). The *quart de rond* is in copper, decorated with shells at the corners; lion-claw feet in chased and gilded bronze.

Collection: Josse (Sold 28 May, 1894, No. 152).

Exhibition: Exposition rétrospective de 1900, *Ameublement*, No. 2888 (No. 1904).

Bibliography: Catalogue, 'Josse Sale', Paris, 1894, No. 39 fig.; Catal. Exposition 1900, p. 188 fig.; E. MOLINIER, *Histoire générale des arts appliqués*, vol. 111, Paris, 1897, p. 99; M. J. BALLOT, 'Charles Cressent, sculpteur, ébéniste et collectionneur', *Archives de l'Art français*, nouv. période, vol. X, Paris, 1919, pp. 106, 113, 136; P. WESCHER, *The J. Paul Getty Museum Guidebook*, pp. 26–27.

CHARLES CRESSENT (1685–1766)

WRITING TABLE ▲

Height: 31 1/2 ins. Length: 76 ins. Width: 38 1/2 ins.

This five-drawer writing table, like the preceding, is decorated with satyr masks on the small drawers. But faun-like faces in the corner *espagnolettes* replace those decorated with female faces. The sides depict the young Bacchus crowned with vine-leaves. An almost identical desk is to be found in the Huntington Art Gallery, San Marino, California.

Collections: Utheman, Saint Petersburg; Sir Chester Beatty. Purchased in 1955.
Bibliography: P. WESCHER, *The J. Paul Getty Museum Guidebook*, pp. 26–27.

Attributed to CHARLES CRESSENT (1685–1766)

COMMODE ▲

Height: 35 3/8 ins. Length: 53 1/2 ins. Width: 25 1/4 ins.

Commode of rosewood, tulip wood and mahogany with slightly curved contours. Two large drawers in the front. A chicory motif in gilded bronze rises from the claw feet and encircles a central panel showing two children playing with a monkey. This motif, with slight variations, is found on several commodes by Cressent. The feet are reminiscent of the work of Gaudreaux.

Collections: George J. Gould (New York Sale, 10 May 1927). Purchased from Arnold Seligmann, Rey and Co., in 1938.

Bibliography: P. WESCHER, *The J. Paul Getty Museum Guidebook*, p. 27.

Attributed to JOSEPH BAUMHAUER (. . . . –1772)

BLACK LACQUER COMMODE ►

Height: 35 1/4 ins. Length: 57 1/2 ins. Width: 24 3/4 ins.

A convex-shaped oak commode overlaid with black and gilt lacquer with floral and animal motifs. The two front drawers are not separated; decorated with gilded bronze floral motifs. Cabriole legs. The top is of veined marble. An almost identical lacquer commode can be found in the Victoria and Albert Museum, London (formerly Jones Collection) and two identical commodes are in the National Gallery of Washington (U.S.A.) (formerly in the Widener Collection).

Collection: Sir Chester Beatty.

Bibliography: P. WESCHER, *The J. Paul Getty Museum Guidebook*, p. 27.

There was, in the ground-floor salon of Mr Chester Beatty's mansion in Kensington Palace Gardens, a splendid commode with lozenge-shaped marquetry studded with bronze rosettes which, to any serious student of eighteenth-century French furniture, at once suggested the work of Joubert, the great *ébéniste* of the reign of Louis XV. I moved the commode to see whether or not the royal cipher was stamped on it, so that I could identify it in the inventory from its number. This commode was put up for sale a few years later. Many people–especially professionals who should have recognized the royal French furniture– walked by it without suspecting what it was. Mr Getty saw it, liked it, reacted to its noble quality and bought it. The discovery that it had been made for the apartment of Madame Louise in Versailles did not, perhaps, come as a surprise to him, but it must have been a pleasant reward.

Another instance of his having been drawn towards the rarest or most sumptuous piece of furniture is the large 'husband and wife' desk which was discovered at the home of the Duke of Argyll in Scotland. The origin of this imposing work will surely be uncovered some day. It can only be an illustrious origin. For which château, for which princesses–probably twin sisters–could such a piece of furniture have been ordered? It was supposedly bought by the Duchess of Argyll in Paris in 1760. So far so good. Without too great a flight of fancy from what was reality, it is possible to imagine that this exceptional piece of furniture was made for two daughters of a king living in cramped quarters in an enormous château, and enjoying a happy reunion

(continued page 151)

B. V. R. B. (Bernard van Riesenberg ?)

◂ 'HUSBAND AND WIFE' DESK ▴

Height: 41 3/4 ins. Length: 62 5/8 ins. Width: 33 ins.

Large double desk, often called 'husband and wife' desk or desk *en dos d'âne*. On the front, marquetry work of flowers and oak leaves; on the sides and interior on the pigeon-hole drawers (see photo above). The cabriole legs are of gilded bronze, as are the mountings, which depict entwined flowering branches. In stressing the rarity of this type of desk, Pierre Verlet has singled out the present example as the 'most outstanding.'

Collections: Purchased by an ancestor of the Duke of Argyll, Lady Elisabeth, in 1760 in Paris. Coll. Duke of Argyll, Scotland. Purchased from Rosenberg and Stiebel.

Bibliography: Pierre VERLET, 'Les meubles français du XVIIIème siècle', vol. II, *Ebénisterie*, Paris, 1956, p. 32; P. WESCHER, *The J. Paul Getty Museum Guidebook*, p. 28. Mentioned and reproduced by André BOUTEMY, 'Les vraies formes du bureau dos d'âne', *Connaissance des Arts*, No. 77, July, 1958, p. 43; Genevieve SOUCHA, 'French XVIIIth Century Furniture', London, p. 55.

B. V. R. B.

◄ TABLE EN CHIFFONNIÈRE

Height: 26½ ins. Length: 13¾ ins. Width: 11 ins.

A small green-lacquer table decorated with blue and gold cross-work on the front, sides, curved feet and central panel; the upper shelf is of Sèvres porcelain with a Dubarry pink background showing *a scène galante* framed in gilded bronze. This plaque, signed 'K. et L.', was made by Dodin in 1761. Mitchell Samuels has called this 'the most marvellous piece of French furniture in the United States'. This masterpiece is of the same type as the famous Guérault table left to the Louvre in 1930, on which the Sèvres plaque bears the date 1766.

Collections: From a private English collection. Purchased in 1949 from Rosenberg and Stiebel, New York.

Bibliography: P. WESCHER, *The J. Paul Getty Museum Guidebook*, p. 29. For comparison, cf. the notice devoted to the Guérault table by P. Verlet, *Les meubles français du XVIIIème siècle*, Vol. II, p. 121.

B. V. R. B. (c. 1740; c. 1770 ?)

◄ WRITING TABLE

Height: 29 1/2 ins. Length: 37 3/4 ins. Width: 22 3/8 ins. at widest.

This small, three-drawer writing desk in rosewood and violet wood, with its especially elegant curving lines, is a masterpiece of Louis XV style. Remarkably fine outline work in gilded bronze with a leaf, flower and rocaille motif.

Collections: Countess of Londesborough, London. Purchased in 1938 from J. M. Botibol, London antique dealer.

Bibliography: P. WESCHER, *The J. Paul Getty Museum Guidebook*, p. 28–29.

JACQUES DUBOIS (1693–1763)

SECRETARY ▶

Height: 40¼ *ins. Length:* 45 *ins. Width:* 14½ *ins.*

Red and gold lacquer, imported from China. The front is divided into three sections: a drop leaf above two doors which open onto shelves. The movable elements on the front are outlined in gilded bronze. The entire front is taken up with a hunting scene in Oriental style with European characters.

Purchased from Rosenberg and Stiebel.

Bibliography: P. WESCHER, *The J. Paul Getty Museum Guidebook*, p. 29.

JACQUES DUBOIS (1693–1763)

CORNER CUPBOARD ▲

Height: 38½ *ins. Width:* 30 *ins.*

A small three-sided piece of furniture with a curved or convex front. Intended for decorating the corners of a room, the corner cupboard is a creation of the eighteenth century and is usually found in pairs. The present example, in ebony, black lacquer and gold, has a single door. The front, framed in gilded bronze, is decorated with chinoiserie (street scenes). The top is of marble. One of a pair.

Collection: Nathaniel de Rothschild, Vienna (Austria). Purchased from Frank Partridge and Sons in October 1950.

after a long separation. When Madame Infanta came from Parma to stay at Versailles in 1749, she was only twenty-two years old. Madame Henriette, her twin sister, died three years later. The dates match perfectly. Louis XV, wishing to give pleasure to the two princesses, encouraged their newly-found intimacy. Might he not have had the idea for this double desk himself, and might he not have ordered the fashionable dealers Lazare Duvaux or Hébert (whose client he was) and their clever *ébéniste Bernard*, to create a new piece of furniture, based on the tilted writing desk, which would allow the two girls to write or arrange their papers without being separated for a moment? Hypothesis or daydream? In any case, the item is of truly regal quality and worthy of the Versailles of Louis XV.

Another item of furniture in the Getty Museum recalls once again the elegance and splendour of the royal châteaux of this period. This is an unusual table, nearly square, with three sliding extensions. It bears–like the desk just discussed–the marking B. v.

(continued page 164)

GILLES JOUBERT (1689–1775)

COMMODE ▲

Height: 36½ ins. Length: 71 ins. Width: 27 ins.

A description of this commode and its companion piece can be found in the Mémoire de tous les ouvrages d'ébénisterie qui ont été faits ou fournis au Garde-Meuble du Roy . . . par Joubert, ébéniste à Paris pendant l'année 1769: '28 August 1769, delivered by Master Joubert for the bedroom of Madame Louise de France at the Château de Versailles: No 2556: Two Regency commodes in rosewood and violetwood with mosaic plaques, having in front two large drawers which may be locked with the same key, and on the sides, two cupboards which may be locked and a shelf within; the panels entirely decorated with small rosettes, the sides with two female busts crowned with laurel and surrounded with double bands of mosaic work; the keyholes, knobs, drop-leafs, rosettes, *souspentes* and feet studded with lion's claws; the whole in chased bronze and very rich ormolu gilding; marble tops, one of Italian and the other of antique marble; 5½ feet long, 24 inches deep and 24 inches high.'

Collection: Sir Chester Beatty.

Bibliography: P. WESCHER, *The J. Paul Getty Museum Guidebook,* pp. 32 and 35; Pierre VERLET, 'French Royal Furnitures', pp. 77 and 111, London, 1963.

JEAN FRANÇOIS OEBEN (c. 1720–1763)

READING TABLE ▲

Height: 28 1/2 ins. Length: 29 1/8 ins. Width: 14 3/4 ins.

Oeben doubtless owed his skill in making mechanical furniture – of which his clients were particularly fond – to his early training as a locksmith. In this *table à glissière,* the action of a key causes the top to slide back and the drawer to come forward, revealing a reading stand. The top is in rosewood, tulip wood, holly and sycamore marquetry with floral ornaments in the centre. The lozenge-shaped decoration on the front of the drawer would seem to indicate a work from the last years of this famous cabinet-maker.

Purchased from Cameron, London, in 1949.

Bibliography: P. WESCHER, *The J. Paul Getty Museum Guidebook,* p. 28.

LOUIS XVI GALLERY (south wall) ▲

from left to right: CABINET, by CARLIN; COMMODE, by G. JOUBERT; SECRETARY, by Jean-François LELEU

On the wall on either side of the mirror: APPLIQUES IN GILDED BRONZE by Pierre GOUTHIERE. Below: GILDED BRONZE ANDIRONS.

Secretary: Drop leaf inlaid with a circular Sèvres plaque having a turquoise blue border enclosing a basket of flowers. The drawer is also inlaid with Sèvres. Fluted legs.

Collections: Hamilton Palace (sale of 1882); Alfred de Rothschild, London.

LOUIS XVI GALLERY ▲

from left to right: MUSIC STAND, M. CARLIN;

WRITING TABLE, Jean-Henri RIESENER (1734–1806). A small and elegant piece of furniture decorated in gilded bronze at the corners and with a surround. *Height*: $26^{3}/_{8}$ *ins. Length*: $21^{5}/_{8}$ *ins. Width*: $13^{3}/_{4}$ *ins.*

Collections: Hamilton Palace, (sale of 1882); Edmond de Rothschild, Paris.

COMMODE 'EN-CAS', Roger VANDERCRUSE, known as LACROIX
A small commode with drawers and sliding doors.

Collections: Duke of Newcastle.
Bibliography: P. WESCHER, *The J. Paul Getty Museum Guidebook*, p. 32.

Height: $36^{1}/_{2}$ *ins. Length*: $23^{1}/_{2}$ *ins. Width*: $17^{1}/_{4}$ *ins.*

on the wall, centre: TAPESTRY, after François BOUCHER

Three personages, a woman and two men, reading music near a wood. This tapestry, known as *La Musique*, comes from a series of *Italian Village Fêtes* for which Boucher did fourteen different drawings and which were reproduced several times between 1736 and 1762, under the direction of Nicolas BESNIER and J. B. OUDRY.

Collection: Ogden L. Mills, New York (Sale of 2 April 1938, Parke-Bernet Galleries, N. Y., Catal. p. 148 and pl. No. 538).

MARTIN CARLIN (c. 1730–1785)

CABINET ►

Height: 46 3/4 ins. Length: 35 5/8 ins. Width: 12 3/4 ins.

Paris, made in 1775

The cabinet, used as a jewel box or medal cabinet, was a specialty of Carlin and Weisweiler and dates from the 18th Century. A counterpart of the present example can be found in the Wallace Collection, London. The door is decorated with a circular Sèvres plaque having a turquoise blue border and a flowerbasket in the centre. The top is of white marble surrounded with a gilded bronze cornice. The top drawer is decorated with draped gilded bronze festoons. The drawer below the drop-leaf is inlaid with Sèvres. The fluted legs are topped with fanciful heads.

Collections: Alphonse and Nathaniel Rothschild, Vienna (Austria).

Bibliography: P. WESCHER, *The J. Paul Getty Museum Guidebook,* p. 33. For the example in the Wallace Collection cf. P. VERLET, *Les meubles français du XVIIIème siècle,* vol. 11, p. 32 and pl. XXIV, 3.

MARTIN CARLIN (c. 1730–1785)

◄ MUSIC STAND

Overall height: 47 1/4 ins. Rack: Height: 12 1/2 ins. Width: 19 3/4 ins.; oval table: Long axis: 15 1/4 ins. short axis: 11 5/8 ins.

Destined for music rooms or for chamber orchestras, music stands can be found as early as the 17th Century, but were most common during the 18th, during which period they were frequently mentioned in inventories. The present example has a large stand with interlaced marquetry pattern enclosed in an oval; candle holders at each side. It is mounted on a three legged table with a single oval shelf. CARLIN executed a music stand for Marie Antoinette which is today in the Victoria and Albert Museum, London. Another can be found in the Cleveland Ohio Museum, U.S.A.

Collection: Sir Chester Beatty, Dublin.

Bibliography: P. WESCHER, *The J. Paul Getty Museum Guidebook,* pp. 33–34.

ADAM WEISWEILER (1752–1809)

DROP-FRONT SECRETARY ►

Height: 47⅝ ins. Length: 32¼ ins. Width: 14¾ ins.

Made in 1780

Secretary of mahogany and thuya wood decorated with chased bronze work by Pierre GOUTHIERE. Caryatids at the corners; upper frieze decorated with a motif of children playing trumpets. The drop-leaf and sides are decorated with white Sèvres porcelain plaques, the former rectangular and the latter ovular, depicting bouquets of flowers. The lower drawer has a motif in gilded bronze of cupids astride lions. The feet are fluted; the top is of white marble.

Collections: Lowengard; Baron Nathaniel de Rothschild, Vienna (Austria).

Bibliography: SEYMOUR DE RICCI, *Le style Louis XVI*, Paris, 1913, p. 127. P. WESCHER, *The J. Paul Getty Museum Guidebook*, p. 33.

MARTIN CARLIN (c. 1730–1785)

◄ CHIFFONNIER or PEDESTAL TABLE GUERIDON TABLE

Height: 28⅜ ins. Diameter: 15⅝ ins.

C. 1775

Round table with two shelves. The upper, basket shelf is decorated with a Sèvres plaque with rose motif. The Sèvres surround is of four *quarts de cercle*. The lower shelf is of rosewood with sunburst marquetry. The feet are decorated in gilded bronze. An identical pedestal table is in the Louvre (Salomon de Rothschild legacy) and another in the former Penard y Fernandes Collection.

Collections: Alfred de Rothschild; Mortimer Schiff (London sale, 22 June 1938, No. 51).

Bibliography: Catalogue of Fine Decorative Furniture . . . of the collection of Mortimer L. Schiff, London, 1938, p. 19, pl. 51. P. WESCHER, *The J. Paul Getty Museum Guidebook*, pp. 33–34. The example from the Louvre is described and illustrated in P. VERLET, *Les meubles français du XVIIIème siècle*; vol. 11; p. 125, pl. XI, 4.

◂ CANAPE

Height: 48 ins. Length: 80 3/4 ins. Width: 29 ins.

Gobelins, c. 1725–1730

This canapé of gilded wood is covered with Gobelin tapestry woven after the designs of Claude Audran and J. B. Oudry. On the back, amidst a decor of landscape and plants, a monkey waves a bow and prepares to play the violin, surrounded by a parrot and a bird. On the seat, a leopard and grotesque animals are surrounded by floral garlands. An extremely rare example of this type of decoration.

Collections: Marquis Boni de Castellane; Georges Blumenthal.

GILDED BRONZE ANDIRONS ▸

Height: 15 1/4 ins. Length: 15 ins.

Period Louis XVI

Chased and gilded andirons decorated on the right-hand side of the base with a garland of grapes and leaves which surround a cup of fruit resting on clouds and surmounted with stars. This base holds a flaming urn decorated with Cupid heads. On the left side, a column surmounted by a pine-cone. On the central bar, crossed trophies. One of a pair. An identical set of andirons was in the former collection of the Marquis de Biron. Another is in the Mobilier National in Paris.

Collections: Clermont-Tonnerre; Mortimer L. Schiff (sale in London, 22 June 1938).

Bibliography: Catalogue of fine decorative furniture . . . of the Collection of Mortimer L. Schiff, p. 16, No. 45. For comparison cf. Catalogue de la Vente Biron, 1914, pl. No. 346 and H. HAVARD, *L'art dans la maison,* Paris, 1884, p. 143, fig. 120.

BERNHARD MOLITOR (maître, 1787)

ROLL-TOP DESK ▲

Height: 53 ins. Length: 68 7/8 ins. Width: 34 ins.

Probably first created between 1760 and 1769 by OEBEN and RIESENER for Louis XV, the roll-top desk with a semi-circular, slatted closing is an outgrowth of the drop-leaf and lean-to desks. The present example is set on thin legs encrusted with gilded bronze; the sides and drawers are decorated with gilded bronze friezes showing vine leaves and cupids blowing trumpets, the work of Pierre GOUTHIERE. When open, the desk has ten drawers and two large pigeon-holes.

Collections: Château de Saint-Cloud (?); Coope; Mortimer L. Schiff (London Sale, 22 June 1938 at Christie's, No. 59).

Bibliography: Catalogue of fine decorative furniture, of the Collection of Mortimer L. Schiff, London, 1938, p. 22, fig. 59. P. WESCHER; *The J. Paul Getty Museum Guidebook*, p. 32.

TAPESTRY ▸

Height: 11 ft. 2 ins. Width: 8 ft. 8 ins.

Gobelins tapestry, between 1728 and 1730

Woven by G. le Blond after the drawings of G. L. Vernausal and Claude Audran le Jeune, this tapestry forms part of a series of ten made for Chancellor Chauvelin. On a royal cloak with a blue background covered with gold *fleur de lys,* surmounted by a canopy and the crown of France, are seen the arms of France and Navarre, in the centre, encircled by the collar of the Order of Saint-Esprit. The Royal initial 'L' alternates with the *fleur de lys* on the pedestal. The border, designed by Claude Audran has, at the four corners, the arms of Chancellor Chauvelin ('Silver, *Chou de Sinople,* a golden serpent on the stalk,'); in the centre, the Chancellor's monogram.

Bibliography: Maurice FENAILLE, *Etat général des Tapisseries de la Manufacture des Gobelins depuis son origine jusqu'à nos jours,* vol. III, 18th century, Paris, 1904, 1st part, 1699–1736, p. 139.

PIERRE GOUTHIERE (1732–1813)

◂ VASE WITH BRONZE GILT BASE

Height: 31¾ ins. Diameter: 16¼ ins. without handles.

Louis XVI

Vase of blue Sèvres with a gilded bronze base decorated with fauns' masks separated by garlands of grapes. The curved feet of the base extend up the sides of the vase in a fluted pattern and terminate at the top in spirals. This base is the work of Pierre GOUTHIERE who had, under Louis XV, the title of 'ciseleur, doreur des Menus Plaisirs du Roy' and who worked up to the time of the Revolution.

Collections: Property of Marie Antoniette. Purchased in 1793 by the Countess Lubomirska during the sale of furniture from Versailles. Count Alfred Potocki Collection (descendant of the Countess Lubomirska), Landshut, Poland, until 1939.

R. B. A similar table–but with mahogany veneer and with a top of pink Italian marble–figures on the list of furniture ordered by Madame de Pompadour from Lazare Duvaux in 1752 for the Château de Bellevue.

The large roll-top desk bearing the stamp of Molitor supposedly comes from the Château of Saint-Cloud, a suggestion which is not impossible. This piece of furniture with ebony and mahogany veneer is decorated on the upper part with a beautiful tablet of red marble. It is of royal quality and magnificence. The bronze work is identical to that which the dealer Daguerre had made for other furniture intended for Louis XVI in the final years of the monarchy, and in particular for the Château de Saint-Cloud.

I think that one can reasonably link Louis XIV with the big Savonnerie carpet acquired by Paul Getty in London at the Mortimer Schiff sale in 1938. This carpet is similar in style to the little-known work done by the *Manufacture de Savonnerie* during the early years of Louis XIV's reign. It precedes the sets ordered by the Sun

◄ SAVONNERIE CARPET ▲

Length: 21 ft. 11 ins. Width: 14 ft. 5 ins.

Period Louis XIV

The carpet is decorated in the centre by an oval cartouche containing a bouquet of flowers; large garlands go out from the central oval, between which are found identical bouquets. Dark blue background; the flowers are cream, yellow, pink, green and brown.

Collections: Georges Kessler; Mortimer L. Schiff (Sale in London, at Christie's, 22 June 1938).

Bibliography: Catalogue of fine decorative furniture of the collection of Mortimer L. Schiff, London 1938, No. 77, p. 29. pl. 77.

King for the Gallery of Apollo or the Grand Gallery in the Louvre, these *ensembles* representing what we know best of the output of this period, notably through what remains of the ninety-three carpets made for the Gallery, also known as the *Galerie du bord de l'eau.* It should be added that few Savonnerie carpets were made before this period and that they are consequently extremely rare. Of the sixty-six carpets listed in the Inventory of Louis XIV before 1667 (the date of delivery of the first carpets made for the Gallery of Apollo), only fifteen originated from the royal works, the rest being oriental. Out of this small number of carpets made either at the Savonnerie of Chaillot or at the Louvre itself, only two have been identified, one of which is in the Getty Museum.

The dimensions of the Getty carpet are unusual for a carpet of this period (21 ft. 11 ins. by 14 ft. 5 ins.). However, it should be noted that it has been cut off at each end. The description reproduced below is taken from the beginning of the carpet inventory of the King. It differs only in the original length given for the carpet (29 ft. 3 ins.), the present width being, given approximately 1 1/2 inches difference, the same as the original. The description which follows is taken from the inventory of the King's carpets, and differs only in the length given:

18. A large new Savonnerie carpet, having a brown background with large white foliate ornamentation and natural flowers; having in the centre an oval cartouche in which is a bunch of flowers with a sun-flower in the middle; having a border also with brown background and with baskets of flowers and vases; seven and one-half ells in length and three and two-thirds ells in width.

These few examples prove that a collector worthy of the name can still—in our own time—find first-class works. To link the names of Louis XIV, Louis XV and Louis XVI with the five pieces we have chosen is to render homage at the same time to the taste of a great art-lover.

ARDABIL CARPET ▸

From the Sanctuary of Safi-ud-Din at Arbadil, Azerbaijan (Persia), 16th Century

Length: 23 ft. 11 ins. Width: 13 ft. 5 ins.

Silk and wool, blue background with floral design. The central medallion of pale yellow terminates in sixteen minaret-shaped points which are prolonged by sixteen insets set off, at top and bottom, by an Arabian mosque lamp on a red background. At the top of the rug is an inscription showing the date of execution: 946 Hegira (1539–1540) by Moqsud Kashani. A counterpart is to be found in the Victoria and Albert Museum, London.

Collections: Clarence Mackay; Yerkes, New York; Capitaine de Lamar; Lord Duveen.

Exhibitions: Persian exhibition, London; Les Arts de l'Iran, l'Ancienne Perse, Bagdad, Bibliothèque Nationale, Paris, 1938; County Museum, Los Angeles.

Bibliography: Catalogue of the Persian exhibition, London, No. 856; *Catalogue de l'Exposition de la Bibliothèque Nationale,* No. 183, p. 188.